The Lifestyle Writer

How to Write for the Home
and Family Market

The Lifestyle Writer

How to Write for the Home
and Family Market

Sarah-Beth Watkins

**COMPASS
BOOKS**

Winchester, UK
Washington, USA

First published by Compass Books, 2013
Compass Books is an imprint of John Hunt Publishing Ltd., Laurel House, Station Approach,
Alresford, Hants, SO24 9JH, UK
office1@jhpbooks.net
www.johnhuntpublishing.com
www.compass-books.net

For distributor details and how to order please visit the 'Ordering' section on our website.

Text copyright: Sarah-Beth Watkins 2013

ISBN: 978 1 78099 984 5

A CIP catalogue record for this book is available from the British Library.

Design: Stuart Davies

Printed and bound by CPI Group (UK) Ltd, Croydon, CR0 4YY

We operate a distinctive and ethical publishing philosophy in all
areas of our business, from our global network of authors to
production and worldwide distribution.

CONTENTS

To my Mum, Julia Barrs-James, for supporting all my lifestyle choices including being a writer.
All my love.

Chapter One

What is Lifestyle Writing?

Look around you. What does your life contain? Home, family, children, grandchildren, eating out, good health, holidays abroad? Or maybe it's not so sunny and your life includes relationship issues, a lack of a decent holiday, imminent surgery and a clapped out car. Wherever you are in your life, whatever you are experiencing, you can turn your life stories into saleable articles for the lifestyle market. People want to read other people's stories. Humans are fascinated by other humans; what they've got, what they are doing, where they are doing it and whether we can do it too!

The Oxford Dictionary describes 'lifestyle' as *the way in which a person lives*. Well, that should provide us with many an idea! Lifestyle magazines include everything from the home and interiors, fashion and beauty, food and nutrition to health and well-being; parenting, childcare, travel and days out are covered too.

What is Lifestyle Writing?

Lifestyle writing focuses on the things that are important in our lives. From raising children, dealing with health issues and being pregnant to decorating your home, managing a city garden and where to go on holiday; writing for the lifestyle market encompasses the aspects of our lives that we can share with other people.

You'll never be short of ideas when you are a lifestyle writer. Everything you do or have done has the potential to be a lifestyle article. If you get stuck for ideas, just talk to your friends and family. What experiences have they had that you could draw upon to write a lifestyle article? Ideas are all around you. Start looking out for them!

Lifestyle writing is one of the easiest markets for a writer to get into mainly because first person viewpoint is often used. This means you can tap into your own experiences to begin your writing career. There are hundreds of magazines that publish lifestyle articles on a weekly basis who eagerly await freelance writers to send in their stories. It's a market you can write for and this book will show you how.

The first article I ever sold was about the differences between the births of my two sons. It started as simply as *'Jake, my first-born son, was born in a hi-tech hospital in Northern Ireland...'* (*Your New Baby, 1997*). That one article for a parenting magazine led to many more lifestyle articles for the same magazine and their website. I began my writing career by writing about pregnancy, child-raising and how to survive as a parent when my children were young. What has affected your life recently that could make a good article?

And what has happened in your past that you could draw on for another interesting article? My latest article was also written from a first person viewpoint and examines my recent foray into making home-made wine. I grew up in a household that produced the most amazing wines from next to nothing and I used this as an introduction to the article.

'My grandparents made home-made wine. They made it from anything and everything: grapes, potatoes, marrows, tea - you name it, they tried it. They started making it during the Second World War and carried it on for many years. As a child I helped pick the grapes and crush them between my tiny toes. Not in a Greek vineyard but in the back garden of a small house in London. We were reared around wine: the smells, the process and later on, the taste.' (*BackHome magazine, 2012*).

When you begin to look at your own life experiences, you will realise that you have just so much to write about. And not just that, but experiences that can help inform, instruct, advise and support your readers too.

Potential Markets

A market is a term used to describe where you can sell your work. So it's not the fruit and veg kind but each magazine, website or publisher is a market where writers can sell their lifestyle articles. There are so many markets out there from magazines and newspapers to websites and e-book providers that it would be impossible to list them all. Lifestyle markets are everywhere, from local publications like Parish journals and community newsletters to national magazines and newspapers and on to global book publishers.

It is estimated that there are 3,300 magazines in the UK and over 10,000 in the US. Magazines are published weekly, sometimes monthly, so that's a huge market looking for writers to fill their pages on a regular basis. And you don't have to just write for magazines in your own country. I live in Ireland and I've sold articles to magazines in the UK, America and Canada so the world really is your market. The best guides for up-to-date information on potential markets are The Writers' and Artists' Yearbook and the Writer's Handbook (UK) and the Writer's Market (US). They contain lists of magazines, newspapers and publishers that you can submit your work to. We'll look more closely at how you can research these types of market in the next chapter.

There are also over 644 million websites on the Internet - someone had to write them! Ok, they may have been initially developed by a computer tech somewhere but they still need writers to produce new articles, website content and blogs for them. Websites are constantly changing, regularly being updated and they need writers to keep them going. Web writing and blogging about lifestyle subjects can be a lucrative market for writers.

Depending on where you find your information, the book industry is stable, unstable or in dire jeopardy. The event of the e-book has changed the face of publishing and there is a huge debate raging about whether this spells the demise of the printed word. I think there will always be a place for both print and e-books and that place will continue to have many lifestyle titles. As well as mainstream book and e-book publishers, the Internet has led to the production of many self-published works. As a writer this means you can produce a book about literally anything and have it available to download directly from the Internet. So if you write a lifestyle book, there will always be a market for it, whether you do it yourself or are contracted to write it.

Why become a Lifestyle Writer?

Why not? There are many opportunities to see your work in print and earn an extra income from your writing. You don't have to commit to writing a book if you don't want to, you can start writing smaller pieces before moving on to bigger things. You can give lifestyle writing as little or as much time as you have available while still building up a portfolio.

Say you have an idea for a book, if you were writing a fiction novel; you would have to complete the whole manuscript before approaching publishers. That's a year; at least, of your time with perhaps nothing to show for it (I'm looking on the negative side here). A lifestyle book, however, starts with a proposal. That will take a few weeks to put together depending on whether the publisher wants one, two or three chapters to go with it but the lifestyle book is commissioned on the basis of that proposal. You don't need to take a year out of your life to write something that may never sell. A lifestyle editor will tell you on the basis of your proposal whether you have a good idea or not. A lifestyle book writer will receive a contract before they have completed the entire manuscript. Your energies and time will not be wasted. If your proposal is no good then you can think of a new idea and try again.

It's the same with articles. A magazine will be looking at features of 1,000 words plus. It's only going to take you a few weeks at most. Once it's in the post or emailed, you start another and your productivity level increases. Web articles can be little as 250 words. That's not going to take long to write, is it? A lifestyle writer can be writing all lengths of factual, informative pieces in a short space of time.

I started my writing career by sending in letters to the editor, tips for advice columns and writing snippets of local news for a community newsletter. I graduated on to writing articles for several magazines. I've written on everything from parenting to wine-making. With the event of the Internet, I started writing for websites and am now a published author. Lifestyle writing can really take you on a journey of many different projects.

And it doesn't matter who you are or where you are, what age you are or what your background is. Writers are a mixed bunch of people. You don't have to be an academic to write about life, everyone has life experiences to draw upon and turn into a saleable article. You don't have to have a posh home to write about interiors or the latest Lamborghini to write about cars; you just need a passion for writing.

If you have hobbies or interests, are a mother or a father, work in a certain industry or are studying for a career, you have life experience that will make interesting articles and lifestyle books. Whatever you do in life has the potential to be turned into a piece of lifestyle writing. So there's no excuses - you can write for the lifestyle market!

But do I need Special Skills?

Not at all. Writing skills improve as you use them; the more you write, the better you will become. You will need a good level of

English to start with and the ability to send in copy that is error free. This might mean going back to the grammar books or punctuation guides to refresh your knowledge of English usage, but these days you can find fun quizzes to test your skills on the Internet or easy to understand books like Lynne Truss's *Eats, Shoots & Leaves* that will update your skills.

Conventions abound around presentation and how to submit your work to publishers and editors. There are ways of laying out articles and human interest stories so that they are editor ready and we will look at those later in this book. Once you have covered the basics, you are ready to write for any publication.

Lifestyle writers do need to be a bit organised though! You will find that research mounts up and will need to be filed. If you start making a good profit from your writing then you will have to keep accounts. You will also want to keep a record of where you have sent your work, on what date and whether your writing was accepted or not. But all this comes as you progress along the path of a writer.

All you need to start with is a love of writing and a desire to share your work and stories with others. A thick skin helps too. Your writing won't always be accepted. Rejections are inevitable for various reasons. Your article might not suit a particular magazine or your book idea might have already been accepted from another writer. Perseverance is the key. As a lifestyle writer, you need to keep writing through the highs and the lows and you will be published. There are so many markets out there that one day your work will see itself in print.

What can you Write About?

You may be an expert in your field of work, an academic with a specific field of study or you may just be a person that has life experiences to share with readers. Whoever you are and whatever you do, you have knowledge and interests to write about.

I said earlier that I've written on everything from parenting to wine-making and, believe me, it's been a wide variety. Some of my articles have included holding Disney-themed birthday parties, writing wedding invitations, visualising your life goals, reading the clouds, homeschooling your teenager and how to choose the best petrol remote control car! Quite a random mix but each one has come from something I was doing at some point in my life. Lifestyle writers really can find ideas in everything they do.

As you go about your everyday chores or working life, think about how you could turn your experiences into lifestyle writing. You go to buy a new car - could you write about what to look for? Or how to get the best deal from a showroom salesman? You've spent the morning at the doctor - could you write about an illness? Or how the health system is failing certain patients? What about that wedding you went to? You could write about wedding trends, fashion, catering, buying presents. Everything you do, however small you may think it is, has the potential to make you a writer. It doesn't matter if the subject has been covered before, if you have a new take on things, can see things from a different perspective or can just write damn good copy, you've got a wealth of experience to draw on.

What are your passions? Do you enjoy gardening, motor sport, football? How about reading, playing computer games and listening to music? Whatever your interests and hobbies are, they too have the potential for you to use them as ideas for your writing. What about your occupation? A landscape gardener could write about how to design a roof top garden, what plants will grow best in a damp garden or how to make cheap and easy pots and containers. A childcare worker could write about fun games to play with kids, what to do on a rainy day or how to encourage children to read. And you don't just have to write about your life. You can write about what others do, what their experiences have been and share their lives with readers too.

Try this Exercise: Chunking down ideas

Answer these five questions:

1. What is (or was) your occupation?
2. What are your hobbies?
3. Where have you lived?
4. Do you have children or grandchildren?
5. Where do you go on holiday or for a relaxing day out?

You now have at least five things you could write about. Now let's focus in a little further.

1. What is the most interesting part of your job? What is the worst part?
2. What hobby or interest are you most passionate about and have knowledge of?
3. Name at least one interesting thing about a place you have lived in.
4. Name one activity you have undertaken with your children or grandchildren.
5. Where was the most interesting place you have visited?

Now you have more ideas about what you could actually write about. Look at each idea to see if it has the potential to be fleshed out as a piece of lifestyle writing.

Is there Money in it?

There are lots of ways to begin making money through lifestyle writing, starting right now. Websites can pay as little as €5 for an article to around €150. Articles can be anything from €30 to €300. Payments depend on each market and, when looking at where to send your work, always check out what the payment rates are.

If you write a novel, it will take you at least a year of your time. If it's fantastic, you may find a publisher who will give you a modest advance and then you have to wait for sales before you see any royalties rolling in. By contrast, a lifestyle book can take less time and so you begin making money a lot quicker. It's hard to gauge the sales of a lifestyle book. It may make you as little as £2,000 but then if it becomes a bestseller, the money will just roll in.

Writers are always told never to give up the day job because, unless you are under contract, you will never know where your next payment is coming from, but there are writers out there that do make a living from their work. It depends on how much you can write and who for. It's like anything in life, the more you put into it, the more you get out of it. Writing is no different. If you commit to being a lifestyle writer, you will gradually build up an income, whether you quit the day job or not.

Where to Find Work

Every time you go into a book shop or newsagents, look at the magazines on the shelves, the newspapers in the rack and the books lining the walls. Many of those will represent a market you can approach. The opportunities are all around you! The next time you read a newspaper or magazine, think about what you could write for them or how you would have covered a subject from a different angle or perspective.

If you already know what subject you would like to write about, check out the specialist magazines that cover your topic. Look to see what books are available and what seems to be missing that might present you with the possibility of writing something to fill that gap.

When you are next browsing on the Internet, see if any of the sites ask for writers to submit their work. Google for writers' sites and find out what paying markets you could sign up to. Once you start looking at the opportunities for lifestyle writing, it will open many doors. Make sure you are ready to step through them, waving a manuscript in your hand!

Chapter Two

The Lifestyle Writer

Before you start writing, there are some things you can do to prepare yourself and get yourself ready to become a lifestyle writer. Reading this book is a good starting point as it will give you lots of tips and advice and hopefully steer you towards a successful career in writing about the subjects you love.

Getting Started

This chapter will help you to organise yourself as a writer, whether that's full-time, part-time or just whenever you have a minute. Organising your space, your writing tools and your time will get you started on the road to becoming a lifestyle writer. Of course you can just pick up a pen and paper or start typing on the computer, but wouldn't it be so much better to get organised so that your writing time really is writing time?

Like setting the mood for a romantic night, you need to set your mood so that you can write. Writers will tell you that procrastination is often their worst enemy. You sit at the keyboard and then think oh I didn't put the washing machine on, the dog needs feeding and I really must order a gift for my aunt then, before you know it, your writing time is gone. You used it up on the everyday chores that we all have to put up with.

So before you get started, make sure you've done everything you need to do and if that little voice keeps insisting on something you have forgotten, write it down and tell it you'll do it later. It's time to concentrate on becoming a writer - let nothing stand in your way.

Becoming a Writer

Deciding to be a writer is a life choice and a decision that will affect your every waking moment. You may have a job that you have to write around or you may be writing because of redundancy or retirement; whatever reason brings you into the world of writing, know that it welcomes you with open arms.

There is work for you if you can commit to it, lots of work on lots of subjects. Magazines, websites and newspapers all want writers, and that includes you. You will need to look for writing opportunities, keep a track of where you send your work and follow up your successes by writing even more stuff, but you can do it.

Start thinking like a writer. Everywhere you go and whatever you do, be aware of potential article ideas. Listen in to other people's conversations - what are they talking about? What are people really interested in at the moment? What's been going on in their lives? An off-the-cuff remark could sow the seed for a great lifestyle article.

Read like a writer. When you read an article in a magazine, ask yourself - what was good about that? What didn't I like? What could have been done better? If this was my writing assignment, how would I have treated that subject?

Also look to see what's not being written about. Say you hear that a new gadget that adverts have been raving about really isn't that good at all, or the gardening season that was going to be so great was devastated by pests, or a new school curriculum isn't going down well with parents - aren't they all topical issues that you could write a lifestyle article about? Sometimes an idea can come from what is missing and ultimately what readers will really want to know.

Part of becoming a writer is becoming aware of what's around you, what people are talking about and what other writers are writing about.

Organising your Area

"A tidy house breeds a tidy mind" - who said that? I'm not sure but it really suits becoming a writer. Ok so your whole house doesn't need to be tidy - I'm not advocating that you become a mr or mrs mop but having a tidy writing area, now that's something.

Pick a place in your home that you can call your own. You might be lucky enough to have an office or study that's ready-made for writing but if not, you need to sequester a space for yourself where you can. It could be a desk under the stairs, a table in the corner of your bedroom or an alcove that would take a few shelves and a writing surface. Somewhere you can keep your computer, files, notebooks and reference material so that it is all close to hand and ready for when you sit down to write.

It won't always be tidy. You should see my writing desk when I'm in full flow; there are papers everywhere, pens strewn about, books open with pens wedged in them as bookmarks and the cat. She's usually in there amongst it all. But at the end of the day, I tidy it up and know that my writing day is done. It can get messy again tomorrow!

What You Will Need

I'm a bit of a stationery collector. I can happily browse an office supplies shop in the same way as some women shop for shoes. I love buying new notebooks, pens and folders in all different colors and patterns to keep cuttings and notes in. I've just bought a lever arch file covered in multi-colored cows and a notebook adorned with butterflies - they just look so good.

Of course, you don't need to be quite as enthusiastic as I am about the basics for writing but you will need some supplies. Your main piece of equipment is going to be a computer. I'm not going to get into technical specifications here, as long as you can type documents on it and preferably have an Internet connection so you can email them out then that's all that you will need. Some writers prefer desk-top computers, others laptops - the choice is yours.

Notebooks are a must but you might prefer to use a tablet

device, your smart phone or a digital recorder. Find some way to record your ideas as you go about your daily life. You could be walking the dog or doing the school run when the most amazing idea pops into your head, if you don't write it down or record it in some way, it's gone. You might also like to flesh out your idea for an article or book on paper before you start typing. I often write down the main points I'm going to cover before I get started. That way, I don't end up staring at a blank computer screen while my brain tries to kick into gear.

I mentioned folders before and a fellow writer told me years ago to always cut out and keep anything of interest I read in newspapers or magazines. They could provide ideas for new articles or contain something that might help with research. So when you're reading, scan for anything that might be of future use and store it safely for when it's needed.

You will add to your writing basics with things like pens, highlighters, paper clips, ink and printer paper as you need them. You might also want a cork-board or a filing cabinet, box files and magazine racks as you progress as a writer. But don't go rushing out to buy the most expensive and unnecessary office equipment, wait until you receive your first writing pay check and then you can treat yourself.

Time and Commitment

Ok, repeat after me - I am a lifestyle writer, I am a lifestyle writer, I am a lifestyle writer... Say it throughout the day, whatever you are doing. It will help you to underline your commitment to writing and to make you feel good about what you are going to do. Writing does take commitment and a good dollop of perseverance.

You need to want to write and more importantly, when you start writing, to commit to finishing the article or book you are working on. Every writer has an amount of started but unfinished work but the key is to actually get some writing finished so you can get it out to editors and publishers.

Writers snatch moments to write whenever they can but if you want to solidly concentrate on a piece of work, you are going to need to find time when you won't be disturbed. I know that is easier said than done if you have a busy household but see where there is a quiet spot during your day. Is it after the kids have gone to bed or before they wake up? Can you fit in an hour after dinner and before you have other commitments? What about your weekends? Can you schedule a few hours out of your time just for writing? Becoming a writer means making time to be a writer. Work out when you will add writing into your life and keep that time specifically for writing and nothing else.

Choosing a Subject

There are loads of subjects you could write about and yes, that old adage says to write about what you know. I say write about what you're interested in because if you don't it will show in your writing and make it dull and uninspiring. You don't have to know everything about a subject you write on but you do need to know enough to write with enthusiasm and authority. I once wrote an article on how to tell if it's going to rain and I'm no weather girl.

'Nature has different ways of letting us know. Woodpeckers and mistle-thrushes sing before rainfall. Rooks and crows fly low to the ground and robins sit on low branches...bees will head back to their homes, frogs croak loudly and cows lie down.' (Scouting magazine, 1999).

I looked at books about nature and particularly, children's nature books as this was aimed at a young readership to give kids things to look out for, things we, as adults, don't tend to notice anymore. My children were small at the time and we went out to test what I had written about. The woodpeckers were missing that day but the cows were definitely keeping their patches of grass dry!

Try this Exercise: The Subject Sheet

Get a sheet of paper and make three columns. Title the first 'subject', the second 'research' and the third '1-5'. Under the subject heading, write down everything you think you could write about, any interests, any experiences, and any topics that you have some knowledge of. Then under the research heading, jot down where you could find out more information. This could be anything from talking to a parenting class to attending a computing conference to visiting a car show. It could be looking up websites, reading reference material or visiting your local library. Be inventive about how you could find out more. Under the third heading, rate each idea from 1-5 (5 being the best) on how comfortable you feel writing about this subject and consider how interested you are in it and whether you would be keen to undertake more research. Circle your 4s and 5s - these are the subjects to start working on.

Realising your Strengths

Only you will know what you feel most driven to write. What is important in your life? What do you feel passionate about? Do you enjoy helping friends plan their weddings or are you amazed at people's health stories? Do you enjoy travelling or are you more of a home bird? Think about what your lifestyle includes and consider how you could use your own experiences to write about these subjects.

I wrote a quick list of what's going on in my life at the moment - raising teenagers, breeding chickens, caring for an elderly cat, researching new vegetarian recipes, making my own beauty products - oh and writing! All of these things have the potential to be written up as articles and in fact, I've already written a web article on the first one!

Your strengths include what you are doing in your life at the moment, what you are involved in, what your passions and interests are and all the elements that make up you and your lifestyle. Take a few moments to think about your strengths and realise what you can start writing about.

Checking the Market

By now, you probably have some ideas of what you might like to write. To help you to decide on what to get started on, look for writing opportunities with magazines and websites. The next time you are in a newsagents, you will see that there are hundreds of magazines and hundreds of markets for you to write for but you will need to find out more about them before you target them with a piece of your writing.

You need to make sure that your article is suitable for the magazine or website that you send it to. There are handy guides that can help you with this information and they are *The Writers' and Artists' Yearbook* and *The Writer's Handbook* for UK writers and *The Writer's Market* for US writers. They contain listings on magazines and newspapers that include contact names and addresses, whether they take freelance contributions, information about word lengths, types of article and the magazine's requirements.

Why does this matter I hear you ask? Well, say you write an article on vegetable gardening and you send it to The English Garden magazine, you'll be sending it to the wrong market. This magazine takes articles on garden design, plant genera and specific English gardens.

If you send your garden article to House & Garden instead, wrong again, only this time it is because the magazine only takes commissioned pieces. If you check out your market first, you'll know what magazine or website takes what kind of lifestyle article.

However, using these guides is no substitute for your own research. Magazines can go out of print, new ones hit the shelves, websites vanish, editors change and so do freelance possibilities. You need to keep an eye on the market for writing opportunities by browsing newsagents, websites and booksellers regularly.

What Magazine?

Go back to your best ideas from the previous exercise and try to find a magazine or website that covers your subjects. You could look in your local bookstore or check out the listings in The Writers' and Artists' Yearbook or The Writer's Market.

List the magazines that you know are available on your chosen topic. For example, if you are a parent and think you could write pieces on childcare, you might come up with *Practical Parenting, Having a Baby, Today's Parent,* etc. Buy some copies of these magazines or borrow them from friends. Libraries and waiting rooms often have a stock you can leaf through as well.

Before thinking of a magazine as a possible place to sell your work, check first if to see if they take freelance contributions. One way is to find the company information; address, telephone numbers, copyright, etc (usually printed near the editorial). Along with this information, it may state something like 'submissions are made at the writer's discretion and the magazine is not liable for the return or use of such manuscripts'. Or it might state that they do not accept unsolicited manuscripts. This means they won't look at anything you send them without being approached with your ideas first.

When you start to write, refer back to the magazine you hope will publish your work. Check that your writing is consistent with their style, word length, tone and that it addresses their type of readers. Make your writing fit so well that no editor will be able to turn you down!

Different Types of Lifestyle Article

There are different types of lifestyle articles; news pieces, factual pieces, informative pieces, reviews, how-to's, humour and personal experiences. When you do your market research, you will see which is most appropriate for the publication or website you are writing for.

For instance, a lifestyle magazine might regularly use 'ten top tips' kind of articles but a website might only have room for five top tips. Some websites only want lifestyle articles that are newsworthy - that means that there is something topical about them - like latest statistics, new products, or this year's holiday destinations. Others might only have slots for first person experience pieces, like how you battled an illness, where you went on holiday this year or what your pregnancy was like.

As you progress as a writer, you will probably write a mixture of articles based on what you know a magazine or website is looking for. If you're lucky, you'll also have an editor contacting you with specific requirements for a certain type of article and you'll jump at the chance to write whatever they are asking for!

Writing a Lifestyle Article

So now that you have some idea of what you might write and where you hope to see it published, it's time to look at how to write a lifestyle article. I will go through some general guidelines here. Not every article will look exactly like my suggestions, some magazines have their own structure that you will see when you - yep, you guessed it - do your market research.

Print articles though generally have three sections; a beginning, a middle and an end. (Check out chapter eleven if you want to write articles for the web - there's a difference!). As well as the main body of your text, you will also need a title and possibly quotes and side-bars.

Titles

Editors can be very fussy about titles. The attraction of titles becomes apparent when you realise that this is what draws you to a magazine and is usually what you scan over when you are deciding whether to buy it or not.

Make your title outstanding. Take time over what you choose. It's going to be the first thing that an editor reads before he or she looks at your article. You need to attract them to your work too. If they have a stack of 25 articles that need reading, whose will be first out of the pile with a snappy title?

Use puns on words, catchy sayings, rhyming phrases – something that stands out and draws you into reading more. Sometimes as little as two or three words can make up the catchiest title. But don't spend more time on your title than you do on your article!

Unfortunately even the best thought out titles can end up on the editor's cutting room floor. They can and will change the title of an article if they feel it's not quite right for the tone of their magazine.

Beginnings

An article's beginning is probably the most important part. It is the hook that attracts the reader, drawing them in and giving them a taste of what's to come. In the first two or three sentences you have to make the intentions of the article clear.

You can start by writing a few catchy sentences or use one of three tricks of the trade. Pose a question that will intrigue readers and make them want to know the answer. The answer is of course contained in the rest of your article but they will be sufficiently interested by the right start to read the whole piece.

'Why is it that once you've had children people expect you to keep producing like some highly successful baby factory?'

'Should we let little kids who have fallen and are hurt pick themselves up – rather than let their teacher comfort them?' (Your New Baby magazine)

Hit your readers with a fact. Use something shocking or startling, something that will make people do a double take. Try things like

In a recent poll, 25% of young adult males said......
One in 10 American women has.....
By the time you're 50 you will have......

You'll either use facts made up from your own research or quoted from an organisation. If you chose to use quotes from reports or statements, you must give the source so you would continue your beginning by mentioning the company, organisation or department that has issued these facts.

Opening up an article with a topical quote can also pull in readers. The more influential or high profile the person or organisation you use a quote from the better. You don't have to only quote the famous. How many times have you read 'a spokesperson for so and so said...'?

Just choose your spokesperson well. Contact managers, directors, professors, doctors – professionals who are experts in their field when looking for a quote.

Quotes

Just remember that whomever you quote you must do so word for word. You don't want to risk legal proceedings over libel and misquoting. Never be tempted to put words into quotes to make them sound better or more interesting. Only use a quote that you know is correct and have a copy of your original transcript or recording on file.

If conducting an interview in person, make sure your interviewee is fully aware that you are recording them or taking notes, that they know who you are and have some contact information like a business card. More on interviewing in chapter twelve.

Of course, quotes aren't just of use in the beginning of an

article. They are invaluable throughout your article to substantiate any claims, back up facts you've used and add authority and weight to a serious piece of writing.

Middle

You've written an amazing beginning, now you need to continue your article. No-one can write it for you so only practice will get it right. Your market research will have told you about word length, style and tone so you have a bare framework to flesh out. Keep paragraphs small and sentences short. Remember to write clearly and concisely. Write tight!

Use the 5 W's - who, why, what, where, when and not forgetting how - to unravel your article. Use any research you have done well. Make full use of quotes and facts, recent studies or developments if they are relevant.

Pace your article well. Say you've got 1200 words to write; perhaps you might use the first 100 in really attracting your reader, the next 200 on the main points, use the body of text to explain the background and unravel the subject and then use the last 200 to sum up.

A word of warning - articles are not essays. Where an essay has a clear introduction, main points and conclusion, articles don't. Articles are top heavy. You want to use your best facts, the most amazing revelations, the crucial information that people really want to know all closer to the beginning than the end. Some people only ever read the first few paragraphs of an article to glean the general information it contains. How many times have you read a feature article because it looked interesting but you never quite made it to the end?

End

That doesn't mean to say you must neglect your ending. Editors are not going to publish articles that trail off indefinitely. Tie up your article by clarifying its overall theme.

Use the last two or three sentences for an upbeat comment for a happy piece, a significant statement for a serious piece. Just wrap it up well so that a reader will feel satisfied that they were right in taking the time to read your work.

Sidebars

Sidebars are added information that appear as a list in a box or separated from the main body of text. They contain information that adds to the article content. They can be used to give the reader details such as contact names and addresses, further reading or websites to look up for more information.

For instance, an article on the virtues of being vegetarian might have a sidebar of recommended recipe books and it might also have a breakdown of essential vitamins. The vitamins could be listed in order of importance with a brief description of their benefits. A sidebar on the dates and times of parenting classes would go well with a piece on child-raising written for a local publication. A list of website designers might go well with an article on designing your own website.

Not every article will need sidebars and this might be dependent also on editorial space but they can definitely add to factual, informative pieces. They are easy to compile and show professionalism on your part.

Keep Going

When you've finished your amazing lifestyle article, send it out, have a five minute break and start another one. (Check out chapter thirteen for help with presentation.) Remember I said you'll need a good dollop of perseverance! Always be thinking ahead about what your next article will cover. If an editor says we love your first article - what else have you got? You need to be able to say this, this and this... keep ideas in your notebook and you will have an answer every time.

Chapter Three

Writing Human Interest Stories

One of the easiest ways to get into lifestyle writing is by writing a human interest story. This type of story is used regularly in magazines and on websites. Editors are always willing to look at new stories that illuminate something incredible, interesting or inspirational that has happened in people's lives.

What is a Human Interest Story?

Human interest stories are articles that cover life's challenges and people's problems, experiences, and concerns. They are stories that come from the heart and elicit an emotional response from their readers. They can often be triumph-over-tragedy pieces, showing how people triumph over adversity and come through the darkest of challenges. For example, it could be a piece on how you overcame a severe illness or how you coped when you were bereaved. Here's an excerpt from a story that I wrote in the form of a letter to my Granddad after he died:

> *You were my dad until I was six, but then Mum got married. We moved to a house in the town just a few miles away but I wanted to stay with you. You always treated me like a father should. I remember frequent trips to the National History Museum and the time you showed me the skeleton of a brontosaurus. "Do you think you are clever?" you asked me. "Yes," I replied confidently. "Well then, tell me how many bones are in that skeleton," you said. I looked in awe at the exhibit and I couldn't even guess.* (Yours, 1998)

The story continues with me explaining how much I missed my Granddad and wished he were still with me. It is one article that

I have written that had a huge response from readers and actually led to me being in touch with one of my Granddad's childhood friends. Although I wrote it primarily for myself, it touched other people's lives and that's what you want from a good human interest story. You want people to feel for the story even if it's written by someone they don't know.

Human interest stories can show outstanding bravery, heroism and achievement like the tales of those who survived Hurricane Katrina or the 9/11 terrorist attacks. This type of story shows how life continues, how resilient we, as humans, really are and they give hope to their readers. These stories can also be used to raise awareness of people that need our help, like a charity or fund that is helping survivors of a tragedy or is researching a cure for a major illness. They can act as follow-ups to events and disasters that otherwise people would begin to forget about.

Human interest stories aren't just about the sadder things in life but they can have a happier twist like the tale of siblings re-united after years apart or an adopted child finding their true parents. It can be so heart-warming to read about how relation-ships endure and how people can find each other after being separated for a long time.

They can also be like mini versions of the stories you hear on *The Jerry Springer Show* - my mum ran off with my boyfriend, my best friend slept with my husband and I don't know who the father of my baby is - a hint of scandal with a dash of gossip. There are some magazines that thrive off stories like this and if you are willing to bare your soul, you can share some of your deepest secrets with their readers.

Humorous human interest stories can cover events that have happened in your life that are upbeat and soul lifting. Everyone wants a laugh and if you can turn your life experiences into humorous articles that will leave your readers with a smile on their face then editors will want to hear from you.

You can also write about life's eccentricities, covering people and their unusual pets, hobbies, collections, etc. Do you know someone who has collected unusual objects for many years, filling their house and garage? Or do you have a relative that has a hippo or an alligator in their back garden? It could be that there's a story in someone's occupation if it is out-of-the-ordinary and unusual in some way. What about a 16-year-old female mortuary assistant or a 75-year-old keep fit instructor? People who challenge our idea of normal and break stereotypes can be great subjects for a human interest article about their lives. I've just read about a cat that lives on an alligator farm and swipes the gators whenever they come too close. So your story could even be about amazing animals too.

Human interest stories are mostly written in the first person. That is from your point of view. This makes them easier to write because you are writing from your own perspective and your own take on your life's events. They still need to be written up professionally but many lifestyle writers begin with this type of article which kick starts their writing career.

Where to find Stories

Human interest stories are all around you. They're in the conversations you have, the events you attend, the people you know and the places you visit. They can also come from what are termed 'hard' news stories.

The next time you read a newspaper, look for ideas for human interest stories. Many of the tabloid papers have small articles that could be investigated more fully for a feature length lifestyle article. It could be a reunion, a natural disaster or an achievement award. If you can source the person involved, they may be interested in having their story written up to appear in a magazine or on a website.

You can also keep ahead of current trends and developments by reading the news. If you are interested in writing about health, a news story on a new form of medication could lead you to writing a healthy lifestyle article. Or you might find out about the release of a new gadget that you could review or fashion trends for the upcoming months that would form the basis of a lifestyle article on the latest craze in clothes.

Using your Own Stories

This is the obvious place to start. But I don't know what to write, I hear you wail! Get your thinking cap on and just consider what you have done over the past week. Have you attended a function? Been to a family member's house for a celebration? Gone to the dentist or doctor? Whatever you have been doing, it has the potential to be written up as a human interest story.

> *"It's 10pm. I've picked the last of the chocolate buttons out of the carpet, cut sticky sweets out of the dog's hair and evaluated the damage to my home after a three-year-old's birthday party. Needless to say, I'm worn out and completely exhausted."* (Your New Baby, 1998).

I wrote this after a memorable birthday party and it led to a series of humorous articles based on my life as a parent of small children.

Try this Exercise: Writing about Yourself

Start thinking about which of your own stories you could write up for inclusion in a magazine or on a website. Consider these questions:

What was the worst relationship you ever had? The best?

When you have been ill how have you coped? What did you do to get better?

What is your best achievement to date? In achieving your goal, were there lessons you have learnt that could be shared with others?

Have you been involved in an interesting hobby or partici-
pated in an unusual fundraising event?

Pick one of these questions and write an article based on your
own experiences. Let your reader know how you felt, what you
did and what the outcome was for you personally.

Remember that when you write a story based on your own
experiences, people are going to read them. That sounds
obvious, but if you say something that your family doesn't like or
you disparage someone in your article, be prepared for the
fallout. I often used my kids as the basis for human interest
parenting stories and as they grew older, they began to hate it.
'Stop writing about us!' they shouted when another copy of a
magazine came out that shared their embarrassing baby secrets.
It's up to you to decide how much you give away but bear in
mind; you might not want to publicize all your secrets!

Writing other Peoples Stories

If you have friends or family with interesting stories to tell, you
can write their stories too with their permission. You can help
them to write in the first person and submit their own stories to
magazines or you can use their stories to write a third person
piece.

Listen with a writer's ear when friends tell you of the troubles
they are having or the amazing things that are happening in their
lives. Even if they don't want to be directly involved in a human
interest story, what they say could give you an idea that could be
written up in a different way.

If they are happy for you to write about them, find out as
much about the details as you can. Use the famous 5Ws - who,
why, what, where, when (and poor old how!) to structure your
article. If you are going for the first person viewpoint, remember
to put yourself in their shoes. Don't be tempted to add in your
own thoughts and opinions. This is their story and not yours so

don't embellish where you think the story could be spiced up.

Payment for this kind of article is tricky. You're really doing this as a favour to a friend. Their name will be on the article and any payment from a magazine will be issued to them although you might be able to agree on a token gift if the article is published. Many people are happy for their stories to be told just to see them in print but others will expect a fee for their contribution. I suggest at this point, if you negotiate an agreement, put it down in writing and have them sign it. You can never be too careful where money is involved.

Interviewing

If you are writing up other people's stories then you will be interviewing them for more information. I know it might feel like you are just sitting down for a chat but this is where you have to make sure that the person you are chatting to really knows that you have every intention of writing up their story and that they are clear that what they say could end up in print.

Your best friend might have told you that her mum has run off with her boyfriend or that she's discovered that her dad is really a woman but you can't just write that up and send it off to a magazine. To put it bluntly, you could be sued for libel and defamation. What's told to you as a secret has to stay a secret unless...

You act as a professional writer. You explain to your friend that her story would make a great article and you'd like to write it up and send it to - and name the magazine, even show them a copy - in the hope of publication.

Ask them if you can get back to them with a list of questions that will form the basis of your article and when you do, conduct the interview professionally. Record what is said via a digital recorder. You can take notes but you will find when you go to write them up that you have missed things or not noted them down correctly. Using a digital recorder means you have everything down word for word and if there is ever any issue about what you included in your human interest story, you have proof.

Gaining Permissions

Always, always gain permission to use another person's story or to quote what they have said. Go one further and before you send in any piece of work, let your interviewee read through your article. They may want to change things, they may have decided not to give as much away or they may be totally delighted you have done such a good job.

When the article is published or it goes online, give them a copy along with your thanks for participating in the article. Keep your interviewees happy and they may come back to you with other stories that you can use.

Is your Story Newsworthy?

Human interest stories don't have to be newsworthy but it can help if you can tie them to an upcoming event or anniversary date. By newsworthy, I mean there is something topical or current about them.

Let's say that there is an award ceremony coming up for adults who have acted bravely in the face of dire circumstances, you could interview one of the people who are receiving the award to tie it into the event. Or there is a high school reunion coming up and you know that two of the people attending were childhood sweethearts who broke up after school but found each other again years later and are now married with kids. There could be a story in how they were re-united that would also publicise the reunion in a local publication.

When a news story breaks, it is often reported with the cold, hard facts. You can use these to investigate further and examine the human element of the story. Controversial news can often lead to great human interest stories - what are the feelings of the people involved? At the time of writing, an abortion clinic has just opened in Belfast. Whatever your views on this subject are, it could lead to an emotional human interest story. Both sides of the debate have compelling stories to tell. Look out for news such as this that could spark a human interest story.

Timing

As well as being aware of using stories when they are topical, you need to remember that magazines often work six months or more in advance. So if you're writing a Christmas article, it needs to go in in the summer - honestly! Websites are much more immediate so you need only work a few weeks in advance but magazines need time to allocate you a slot in their pages.

If you are writing a follow-up to an event, it will also need to go in way before the actual anniversary date. Don't submit a story about how survivors are coping one year on, two weeks before the remembrance of the date. Plan your writing so that a magazine has plenty of time to use your work in their pages. Check with the editorial team as to how far in advance they need topical human interest stories and you will know when to submit your work.

Making your Readers Feel

Human interest stories are all about making your reader feel for the person or people involved in your story. Mood and emotion can be created by writing good descriptive passages that show your reader, rather than telling them. This is something that writers hear over and over again - show, don't tell.

Stories are driven forward by the acts, thoughts and deeds of the people telling the tale. So in writing what you or the main person in your human interest story was doing, you should show your reader not tell them. Here are some examples:

Telling: I was unhappy.
Showing: I wiped the tears from my eyes as I read his letter.

Telling: I was so excited.

Showing: I ripped open the wrapping of the gift he had given me.

Your reader wants to experience your story through your eyes so, whatever is happening, the reader wants to be able to visualise it. Telling them does not engage them emotionally in your writing. Telling just gives them information and it can make the reading experience boring. Showing, however, helps your reader to experience your story as if they were there. To make sure you are 'showing' when you write, use action, dialogue and the five senses to move your story forward.

To create an emotional bond between your readers and the story they are reading, the individual that the story is about must be believable and interesting enough for your reader to care enough about finding out what happened to them. Especially when you are writing about yourself, take care to add in enough detail so that someone who is reading your human interest story gets a sense of who you are and why they should be interested in finding out more about you.

We have previously talked about using quotes if you are writing up someone else's story and these will be given to you at interview stage. You want to pick the most interesting and compelling quotes that not only make your writing more authentic but move the story forward. It's the same when you are telling your own story; include dialogue that gives the reader essential information and helps to give them a sense of atmosphere. You don't need to include long passages of dialogue but, like in the example earlier in this chapter of my conversation with my Granddad, you can add in a few lines that give a sense of the relationship between people that will move the story along.

Who Publishes Human Interest Stories?

Lots of magazines use one or two human interest stories per issue especially those that are targeted at specific subjects. Parenting magazines often carry birth stories, car enthusiast publications have stories about rebuilds, travel mags have stories about readers' holidays and health and wellbeing publications carry loads of first person experience stories.

Some magazines publish nearly all human interest stories and these can be lucrative markets to target. UK magazines like Take a Break, Bella, Best, That's Life and Chat and US magazines like the People, Breathe, Sasee and More all publish human interest stories in every edition and they actively look for stories, paying good sums of money for them. They may take your work as is or phone you for more information to add into the article which is then re-written by a member of staff - but you still get paid.

The next time you are browsing the magazine racks in your local store, look out for the ones that take human interest stories. You might just have a story to suit.

Chapter Four

Writing Parenting and Childcare Articles

If you've raised children, worked in a childcare setting or have been involved in a youth organisation, you have experience that you can tap into to write parenting and childcare articles. This is a huge market for freelance writers with parenting magazines being published in their hundreds. Some deal with just pregnancy, others are aimed at the family, while yet others focus on working mums or green parenting. There is some variety between the magazines so if you are interested in this topic, grab some of the latest copies and start perusing.

From 0-18 years

Childhood covers the early years, through school age and onto the teenage years. There are opportunities to write about parenting and child-raising at every stage of a child's development however most of the parenting magazines have a fixed target group.

Baby and parenting magazines tend to include articles that cover the pre-school years or roughly 0-5 year olds. Family orientated magazines carry articles for older children and some go as far as the teenage years. Some magazines have a particular focus like green parenting or being a working mum and so anything you write needs to be tailored to their specific readership.

Parenting covers so many topics; health and safety, medical advice, crafts, cookery, education, coping with childhood illness, breast-feeding, what to expect in hospital, baby toys, pregnancy difficulties, birthing classes, baby names, what to do when your child starts pre-school, what to do when your toddler swears...phew, the list is endless. You've got some ideas too, right?

Try this Exercise: Parenting Stories

If you are a parent or grandparent this will be easy. If you don't have kids of your own but have worked with them, you might have to think more outside of the box. Try these questions anyway to see if they generate some ideas.

What happened in your pregnancy that you didn't expect?
Did you plan for a certain type of birth and did things go according to that plan?
What was your child's favourite game as a toddler?
What is the most important piece of advice that you would give a friend if they were pregnant for the first time?
What did you enjoy doing with your child when they were 5, 10 and then 15?

Select one of these ideas and look at some parenting magazines to see which one your article would suit. Then get writing!

Starting with Pregnancy

Pregnancy is such a life-changing event in a woman's (and man's!) life that some magazines focus particularly on this nine month period and having a newborn baby. This type of magazine is packed with readers' stories but also lots of practical tips and advice articles to help new mums cope with their pregnancy and prepare for the birth of their child.

Pregnancy magazines not only deal with pregnancy and birth, they also cover information on pre-pregnancy, like how to eat healthily before conception, what to do if you can't conceive and how to tell if you are expecting.

Think about what advice you could share with other mums. What did you do to relieve an aching back? Did you attend birthing or parenting classes? How did you juggle work with pregnancy? Delve into your own experiences for some great article ideas.

As well as first person stories, these magazines use full-length factual articles. Start by working on an idea that you have some knowledge and experience of. For instance, I used essential oils during pregnancy to great effect. I used my experience to write an article that helped mums to relieve some of their pregnancy niggles using essential oils.

"In today's ever progressing world, it's nice to go back to our roots and treat ourselves with something natural. Essential oils not only smell divine but can also alleviate pregnancy complaints in the nicest possible way... Morning sickness and bouts of nausea can make early months a misery. Spearmint oil helps combat sickness and settles the stomach but you don't take it internally. Place one drop on your pillow or if this smells too strong, leave a bowl of warm water with three drops in by your bedside so that the subtle aroma can work overnight." (Your New Baby, 1999).

I went on to list oils that could be used for constipation, leg cramps, tiredness and stretch marks and how to use them. I also included information on what oils were safe to use in pregnancy and which oils were not, as well as information about stockists and further reading.

Investigate and research an area of pregnancy to write a more in-depth article. Say you had morning sickness, could you write a piece about the different remedies that are used? What about remedies that are used in other cultures? How about pain relief? Are there any new forms of pain relief or are women still using traditional methods? Factual articles that give prospective mums detailed information about pregnancy and birth are always welcomed by magazines who need new ideas and articles on a regular basis.

All about Birth

Birth stories are some of the most popular articles. Magazines regularly use readers' stories and it gives mums a chance to share what they went through. Every birth story is different so don't be afraid to share yours. In chapter one, I mentioned that my first article was a birth story but it wasn't just about the birth of one child. It was about the difference between births - one surgical and the other natural. It ended on an uplifting note so women that had traumatic births wouldn't be afraid to conceive again.

> *"Jake's delivery taught me that pain and trouble walk hand in hand at birth - but my second son, Shay, proved me wrong and now I can't wait to try again!"* (Your New Baby, 1997).

Whether you gave birth in hospital, at home or somewhere totally unexpected, you have a story. The methods you used, the pain relief you tried, the people that surrounded you; they all make great elements for a birth story.

Education and Homeschooling

Education doesn't just start with school; lots of parenting magazines cover topics such as how to help your baby to enjoy books, how to help them learn new words and having a bi-lingual baby. Once we range towards the nursery years, we start to find articles about preparing your child for pre-school, what you can do to help them learn and what to do if your child doesn't like pre-school.

There is plenty of scope to write educational articles and you don't need to be an expert. If you have experience of teaching a child or of helping them to cope with learning difficulties, you have the basis for an article. You don't need to write academically because your readers are going to be mums that are looking for advice and support. Come up with practical tips and sound information that can help a child's learning process.

A lot of articles focus on supporting your child's education and helping them to manage in the school system but in recent years, there has been an increase in children who are homeschooled. This is another area where you can concentrate your writing and come up with tips and ideas for educational activities for various ages. If you are a homeschooler yourself then you could write about how it has worked for you and your child, the ups and downs and the issues surrounding homeschooling. Just bear in mind that laws regarding homeschooling vary from country to country so if you are writing about, say the registration process you went through, it may not be appropriate to sell it to a magazine outside of where you live.

What about Arts and Crafts?

I love writing about arts and crafts ideas for children. When my boys were small, I read this kind of article and tried out many new ideas to fill a rainy afternoon. When I began writing this type of article, I tested them out before writing them up. Some provided hours of fun and others were disasters but we had great fun seeing which was which.

Arts and crafts can be tied into occasions and special days so you can write about fun things to make for Christmas, Thanksgiving, Halloween, Easter - whatever your family celebrates. You can also write general pieces like painting ideas, what to make with paper or how to use clay with little ones.

When writing articles like this check that any instructions are child-friendly. By this I mean if it includes using scissors you mention children's ones or alert the reader to a part of the process that will need an adult's help. If there's preparation needed, tell the readers what to get ready so young children don't get bored waiting for clay to harden or paper mache to soak. Make your instructions as clear as possible and stick with non-complicated crafts that are appropriate for the magazine's age range.

Cookery for Kids

Try out some recipes at home and write them up for a kids cookery feature. This can provide hours of fun and mess for you and your child but also give you the basis for a great article. Break your cookery exploits down into step-by-step instructions and include an ingredients list if needed. None of the recipes you use should be complicated. Although kids love cookery, they get bored easily and so you want to write about quick and easy things to make.

You need to be careful with recipes that include baking, cutting or heating and signal to mums (and dads!) what they need to do and what their child can help out with. For instance, I wrote an article about spending time in the kitchen with your toddler that included several cookery ideas including making animal crackers.

> *"Take a packet of cream crackers, a tub of soft butter and some thin cheese slices. Decide what animal to make. Let's say a pig - mum or dad could cut a round for the face and small triangles for the ears and let the child arrange them on the cracker using butter or marg to stick down. Use a cherry tomato chopped in half for the eyes, a cucumber with two small holes cut out for the nose. Your child can spread the butter and make the face; you get to do the cutting and chopping."* (Your New Baby, 2002)

It might seem like you are stating the obvious but editors want articles that take into consideration a child's safety.

You can also use cookery ideas in articles about celebrating special occasions like birthdays. Mums might like easy-to-make ideas for birthday cakes, healthy party snacks and non-calorific drinks. Or what about an article about making your own baby food? For health-conscious mums, a piece on organic baby food preparation could be a blessing. You could write articles containing nutritional advice; what about babies with specific dietary requirements? I once wrote an article about raising vegetarian babies. Mums who have babies that are vegan, lactose intolerant or have food allergies will love articles that give them new ideas for meals to prepare and information on how to ensure that their baby is receiving all the essential vitamins and minerals they need.

Writing Top Ten Tips

Another type of article that is popular with pregnancy and parenting magazines are the 'top ten tips' style of article. You come up with a list title - I've used things like *10 ways to cope with being a new mum, 10 good things about being a mum* and *10 top energy tips for mums-to-be* - then list each point 1-10 making each one an easy-to-follow advice tip.

Lists are written in an informal chatty style often using the second person viewpoint 'you'. They can be factual or they can be humorous and aimed at giving readers a laugh about what is usually a serious subject. You can draw on your own experiences or chat to other mums for their ideas to fill out your lists.

Don't forget Dad!

Writing about pregnancy, birth and parenting doesn't have to come from an all female point of view. Dads have views, opinions and experiences too. One magazine I used to write for had a regular column that was written by a dad so readers had a male perspective too.

You could interview some dads for a feature article that includes what they found scary about pregnancy and birth or how they coped with being a new dad. Whatever you are writing, consider whether including a male viewpoint would make interesting reading. Dads need advice sometimes too!

Writing about Teens

Writing about teenagers can cover some tricky issues. Parents want to know what has happened to their lovely, cheerful, little babies that now have a mind of their own and a mouth to go with it. Not every teenager turns out to be the one from hell but the teenage years can be difficult for all involved.

Issues like drugs, drink, sex and dating come round generation after generation. Times change and so do our attitudes and our concept of what is acceptable and what is not. If you look at articles about teenagers that were written ten years ago, you'll find they gave advice to parents that differs from the advice that is given today.

Not all parenting magazines go as far as the teenage years and you will want to check your markets to find which magazines or websites would be interested in a teen piece. I've just written a short article on how to raise teens for a website, drawing on my own experiences of raising two teenage sons, so the opportunities are out there if this age range interests you.

Writing for Them

There is a market for teenage advice pieces. They aren't found in parenting and childcare magazines but in the pages of magazines specifically for teenagers. If you can remember what it was like to be a teenager, have reared your own and can write in a way that is suitable for today's teens then you could check out this market.

Have a look at teen magazines and websites to see if there are any openings for freelance writers. You don't have to be a teen to write teen advice but you do need to write articles that speak to teenagers on their level. They don't have to be simple, the last thing teenagers want is to be spoken down to and they definitely don't want to read anything that sounds like a parent has written it.

If you want to try writing for teens, keep your writing talkative and informal. Don't pick a topic that has been overdone. In the previous section, I mentioned the subjects that parents want to know about; drinks, sex, drugs - but teens don't want to read about these overdone subjects unless it's from a completely new perspective or has a different slant to it.

To find out what really matters to teens and what advice they actually want, you need to talk to them. As a writer, you need to know exactly what teens are facing these days, what their issues are, what problems they have and what kind of world they are living in. You might think it is the same as yours but start talking to teenagers and you'll be surprised at how much they know and what it's really like to be a teenager in the 21st century.

Using your Own Stories

In the last chapter, we looked at using your own stories to write human interest pieces and you can also delve into your own stories to write about pregnancy, birth and child care. Ideas for factual articles may stem from your own experiences and this is fine but be clear on what you are writing. Your own story will be written in the first person whereas a factual article will be written in the third person. Most magazines have very specific slots for first person stories but the majority of their articles will be of the informative and detailed third person type.

You can still add in quotes if they are relevant to the main body of your text. Keep them short and always acknowledge the person or organisation that gave you the quote. Put the quote in speech marks and also italics if the magazine requires it.

Protecting Identities

We've talked before about gaining permissions and it is equally important to make sure that any mums or dads you interview for your writing are fully aware that their words may be quoted. Sometimes parents will want to protect the identities of their children, especially if you are writing about teenagers or an issue that has caused a child some distress. In this case you can say that they wish to remain anonymous or you can change their names.

Photos of children also pose problems and you may need signed permission to photograph children for an article. You won't always need to accompany an article with a photo but many websites require a small image to be uploaded with them. You can use stock photos from sites such as www.flickr.com or www.morguefile.com but always ensure that these are appropriate for commercial use and that you comply with any rights that the photographer has reserved.

Some of the Top Magazines

Magazines come and go. Some stay in print, others become online versions. If you are interested in writing for the parenting market, keep ahead of what magazines and websites you could write for. Have a few copies in your files so that you can check them for style, length and content before you submit your own work.

Here are some magazines to look out for. In the US:

American Baby
Parenting
Family Fun
Fit Pregnancy
Kiwi
Parent and Child
Parents
Pregnancy & Newborn

And in the UK:

Practical Parenting
Mother & Baby
Pregnancy, Baby & You
Junior
Green Parent

ABC
Prima Baby & Pregnancy
Happy Families
Pregnancy & Birth
Juno

Chapter Five

Writing about Health

Health is a subject that appears in parenting magazines, women's magazines, men's mags and on websites, as well as having its own magazines especially dedicated to all things health. Everyone wants to live a healthy lifestyle but we aren't all saints neither are we all blessed with perfect health. These magazines offer advice, ways to cope with illnesses and ailments, information on new remedies and fact packed articles and for the professional, up-to-date information about their area of work.

What can you Write about?

The topic of health covers a huge range of subjects and this can be seen in the varying types of health magazine that are available. There are magazines that deal with general health and wellbeing, health conditions, elderly care, nursing, psychology, pharmaceuticals, healthy eating and nutrition, pet allergies, natural health, dieting, exercise...you name it, it's there. Health magazines range from those intended for the general public to those aimed at professionals in their field. Articles can be easy-to-read or far more academic and in-depth, giving you as a writer a range of possibilities to choose from.

Do you need to be an Expert?

This is a yes and no answer. You don't need to be an expert to write about your own experiences or to write general health pieces but if you were writing about brain surgery, medical procedures or nursing equipment, you would be expected to work in those professions and have an academic knowledge as well as practical experience.

There is a middle ground of people who have perhaps trained

as counsellors or have taken alternative therapy qualifications. I am a qualified life coach and NLP practitioner and have written on those subjects for a few websites and magazines. This excerpt from an article about combining life coaching, CBT and NLP was written for www.worldwidehealth.com.

"Life coaching, cognitive behavioural therapy and neuro-linguistic programming can work together in any client situation. They act as tools to help improve and change a person's life. Many practitioners specialise in one specific area but they can be combined to give the client a more powerful and successful outcome and the practitioner a wider range of tools and technologies to use."

At the end of this article there is a list of my qualifications so that readers know that I have at least a vague idea of what I'm talking about!

Do you have any skills or qualifications relating to health that you could use to back up your stories? It could be anything from aromatherapy to hypnotherapy or using Bach flower remedies. Have you been involved in a fitness class, managed a weight loss group or worked on a healthy eating project? These kinds of life experiences can give you extra kudos when approaching editors with healthy lifestyle articles.

Holistic v. Medical

There is a big difference within magazines on whether they focus on holistic or medical stories, information and advice. Women's magazines might take a mixture of the two especially with readers' stories but other magazines tend to lean one way or the other.

Medical magazines target those working in the profession and contain more academic material on its topics. They usually cover things like new product reviews, the pharmaceutical sector, latest studies and regulatory updates. Check out magazines like Modern Physician (www.modernphysician.com), Doctormag (www.en.doctmag.com) or Biomechanics (www.bio mech.com) for examples of what gets published in these more academic magazines.

Alternative health or holistic, natural health magazines cover topics like vitamins and supplements, recipes and home remedies, herbs, healthy living and information on general wellbeing. Take a look at magazines like Natural Health (www.naturalhealthmag.com), Healthy Living (www.healthyliv ingmagazine.ca) and Natural Solutions (www.naturalsolu tionsmag.com) to see the difference between these types of magazines.

If you are hoping to write about health, you need to consider whether your writing strengths lie more with medical or holistic articles.

Try this Exercise: Medical or Natural?

Think of a time when you weren't well. Say you had a bad back or the flu, what did you do to cure it? If you went to the doctors and received medication, look up what alternative remedies you could have used. If you went to the health food shop and stocked up on supplements and did back-stretching exercises, look up what medication you could have been prescribed instead.

Use this exercise to look at the two different sides of health care (of course, in real life many people mix the both) and examine where your interests lie and which type of remedy you usually go for. Try writing a short article from both points of view. Which is easiest to write? This exercise will help you to decide what type of health articles suit you and what you could concentrate on writing.

Surgery Stories

Oooh, gross! If you are squeamish like me, this is the last thing that you want to read or write about but some magazines regularly take this type of article and ask their readers to send in their personal stories. The purpose of this kind of article is to explain a procedure but also to show how a reader coped with their surgery and what they did to recover. They aim to help anyone that is going to go through similar surgery to feel ok about what they will be going through and to know that not only have other people gone through the same process, they have come out the other side feeling fit and well.

These are not doom and gloom stories. No one wants to read about a surgery that had complications and has left the person in pain for the rest of their years. They are more uplifting than that. There may have been complications but what was done to get over them? Were alternative remedies used? What are the positives that have happened as a result of the surgery?

Some people make life-changing decisions after major surgery. It could be that their lifestyle has to change as a direct result or that they have had to re-evaluate their lives because of their condition. Has someone you know changed their career path after surgery or decided to go on a journey or take up an interesting hobby because of what they went through?

Surgery stories are usually written in the first person but, as with human interest stories, you can write up another person's story in the third person on their behalf. Or you can just write up your own experiences but remember, no matter how bad it was, end on an uplifting note.

Looking at Wellbeing

What is wellbeing? My dictionary says it's the state of being comfortable, healthy or happy. So that includes a huge range of possible topics! As an example, the website, Complete Wellbeing, covers topics such as therapies, relationships, the mind and emotions, spirituality, health and healing, the body and beauty, nutrition and everyday wellbeing. Look at their guidelines for writers to see what type of writing a wellbeing website looks for at www.completewellbeing.com/for-prospective-writers.

Wellbeing is not only about having a healthy body; it's also about having a healthy mind. I recently wrote a short visualisation piece for a health magazine. You could even try it out yourself!

One of the best ways to achieve your life goals is to focus your mind with a life purpose visualisation. Find time to relax, close your eyes and imagine yourself in a very plush hotel. You have been asked to attend a prestigious award-giving event. You are sitting with friends and family right at the front, waiting for someone to come to the podium. When they do, they announce the main award. As everyone starts applauding, the award winner comes to the podium. It is you in the future!

Let your mind imagine what you say next as you give your acceptance speech. What is it for?

What have you achieved? How does this make you feel? Feel yourself accepting the award, thanking the people who have come here especially to see you and absorb your accomplishment for a few moments. Carry your feelings of achievement around with you as you work towards your goal. (Natural Health, 2012)

Writing about wellbeing can include lifestyle articles about organising your goals, achieving your life's purpose and how to make changes in your life. They can use theories from psychology or techniques such as the ones that coaches and NLP practitioners use. If you have any experience of these, think about using them in for a wellbeing article.

Relaxation and Stress Management

Articles covering relaxation and stress management have become more important in recent times as our lives increasingly become busy. The top ten stress factors in our lives are:

The death of a spouse or partner
Divorce
Being sent to prison
Separation
Death of a close family member
Major personal illness or injury
Getting married
Redundancy or being sacked
Retirement
Major illness of a family member

Stress can also come from pregnancy, work, your finances, a career change, your children, moving home and other areas. Editors want articles that help their readers to beat stress in new ways. Many of the obvious relaxation techniques have been covered, like breathing techniques, self-hypnosis, work-stress management and work-life balancing, but if you have new ideas or have tried out new therapies or techniques, you could have the makings of an article that will not only make you money (relieving financial stress!), it will help out someone who needs help with the stresses in their lives.

Exercise and Diet

Many health magazines also carry articles that cover exercise and diet. There are tips and exercises to increase your fitness levels and recipe ideas for nutritional, healthy meals. If you have an idea for this type of article, make sure it is appropriate for the magazine of your choice. There are also magazines that concentrate on specific diets like vegetarian or vegan or cover diets for particular conditions like diabetes. If you have specialist knowledge or have your own life experiences of following such a diet, then look for magazines and websites that focus in on them.

Two examples of diet magazines are the Vegetarian Times

and Vegetarian Living. The Vegetarian Times (www.vegetariantimes.com) has recipes, expert wellness information and environmental lifestyle articles. They say that their goal is to provide health-conscious, eco-friendly, "green" lifestyle writing. Vegetarian Living (www.vegetarianliving.co.uk) is a similar magazine and you can contact them with any ideas for stories or recipes via their website.

Have a look in the magazine racks for titles that cover the type of exercise you like or more importantly, that you could write about. There are magazines for yoga enthusiasts, walkers, cyclists, and other physical activities that people are involved in. For example, body building and weight training magazines focus on topics for people involved in this particular type of fitness. Magazines like Muscle and Fitness, Flex, Powerlifting USA and Iron Man contain articles that inform readers of how they can follow a body building lifestyle.

Because these magazines are so specific, they often need articles with up-to-date information on a regular basis, providing opportunities for you, as a lifestyle writer, to get cracking in this market.

Writing for the Mind, Body & Spirit market

This market is a huge area of growth in the writing and publishing industry as more and more people look more deeply at their lives. In a recent copy of Natural Health magazine, their Mind articles included how to find your inner strength, natural ways to beat stress and the top five stress-busting foods. Body articles included ten chemical-free lipsticks, how to tune into your sexual energy and how to keep your heart healthy. The Soul section had articles on how to be a sun goddess, how to boost your creativity and where to go for a retreat. As with writing about health in general, the mind, body and spirit (or soul) market covers a range of articles.

The book industry is even more diverse. New Consciousness

Review (www.ncreview.com) is a website aimed at reviewing all the latest books in this genre. Check them out to see what kind of books are being produced at the moment and what publishers you could contact if you have an idea for a mind, body and spirit book. (We will look more closely at writing lifestyle books in chapter fourteen).

Try it Yourself

As I suggested with writing about crafts or cookery for the parenting market, you can try out healthy things for the sake of an article. Now don't tell me you don't want a massage, aromatherapy session or spa day? Of course, you will have to pay for the costs of your treatment but if your article sells it should pay for itself - unless you booked in for a weekend at the most exclusive resort in your area!

Look out for health fairs or days in your locality. They often give out free samples that you can try or offer quick trial sessions with therapy providers. You might find something here that would warrant further investigation and then be written up as an article.

Having a Column

I've always wanted to be an agony aunt. How cool would that be? You get to read through readers' letters and offer up advice in your very own writing column. There was a time when this really seemed to be the forte of women writers and the jobs were offered out to journalists and writers who had some connection with a magazine.

Nowadays you need to know your stuff and that means being qualified in a related field. Columns are now written by counsellors, psychologists, life coaches, doctors and people who are experts in their field, who have experience of working with clients and have a background to prove it.

Column writing jobs are hard to come by. They are hardly

ever advertised and it seems to be a case of who you know. If you do have the relevant qualifications and an idea for a column though, there's nothing to stop you from contacting a magazine or newspaper with your idea. Send in a query outlining your expertise, your idea for a column and what topics you think will be covered. Add in some examples or a mock-up of what questions you think you'll be asked and what your responses would be. If editors are looking for new columnists and your background and writing skills fit, you just might be in with the chance of a new job.

Writing for Therapy

When I was tutoring a course some years ago, one of the participants told me that he was dealing with a major illness and he didn't know what the outcome would be. He had decided to write about his experiences as a way to get through the pain, to give his life some purpose and to try to make sense of it all. I encouraged him to write a range of articles and to put himself in the position of an observer when he had any treatments so that he could write about them afterwards. I'm delighted to say that he fully recovered and became a writer for several health magazines. He used writing as therapy and it had great results.

I'm not saying that you need writing therapy but there are times when every writer needs to work out their own personal issues. There are some techniques you can use to help you in this way. You can also use these techniques as the basis for a health article if you decide that you would like to share your thoughts with the general public. Try writing:

Diaries

Many of us had them as teenagers, some of us still have them now but have you ever really written your true feelings down? Often we write in our diaries of events that we've attended, parties, and holidays but have we really used them to explore our emotions?

Start now by exploring your emotions in a diary on a daily basis. If your boss made you angry or your partner made you cry, describe how you felt and why you were so upset. Then ask yourself why you were so upset again. Often an incident makes us mad or sad but what else is going on? If we allow ourselves expression, we can see what else is behind our reactions.

A diary also serves as a record. You might begin to see a pattern of when you are low or when you feel the greatest. Does your mood dip if you haven't eaten breakfast or skipped lunch and just drank coffee? Diaries can help us log our emotions and see if there are underlying factors.

Poetry

You don't have to have any knowledge of stanzas or iambic pentameters to write a poem. Poems help by letting us pour out our emotions in words and phrases rather than full sentences. Sometimes they help when you can't make sense of what's going on by just jotting down immediate feelings. List poems are also great for getting things off your chest. Think of an issue that is getting to you and write each line as an aspect of it.

Freeflow Writing

Freeflow writing is when you let out anything that is going on in your head through your pen. Give yourself a time limit, say 10 minutes, and just write anything that comes to mind. It doesn't matter what it is or whether it makes sense or not. Just let it all out.

If you like, you can come back to it and go through it, to see if any issues are showing themselves. Pick out the sentence that you wrote that feels full of emotion. Use it to start another freeflow writing session, again timed for 10 minutes. Keep working on that issue over a week or two until you feel like you have written it out of your system.

Dialogue

This can be very effective when you have had a conversation but wished it had gone another way or when you haven't been able to get your point across. It's also a good method to help you talk to someone you have lost and to say those things that were left unsaid.

Imagine you are talking to the person who you still need to speak to. Write down what you would say and imagine how they would respond. Work through the conversation until you have said what has been on your mind. Let them give the responses you need to hear while freeing yourself of the words that have been bottled up.

Dream Journals

Dreams are our subconscious mulling over recent events and deep seated emotions. Some people can't remember their dreams, others have vivid nightmares. Keeping a dream journal can help you to see what your mind is working on. Try recalling your dreams as soon as you wake up and spend a few minutes jotting down what happened in them before you start your day. Are they trying to tell you something?

Autobiography

Your life story or parts of your life can be written like an auto-biography. Look at the bestseller lists and you'll see many books that have been written about trauma, unconventional childhoods and problematic upbringings. You don't have to go as far as publication but it can be extremely therapeutic to write down experiences in your life as you experienced them. You don't have to show anyone else but they could make great articles.

Lists

Positive writing creates positive thinking. Lists are great for quick pick me ups. Try the 'I love myself because...' or 'My life is great because...' Do them when you don't feel great to remind you of all the good things in your life, even when times are hard. Before you go to bed, jot down five things you have been grateful for during your day. This can help you to see the good in what you might have thought was a bad day. I bet you can always come up with more than five and if you do, it could make for a great top five or ten list to send into a magazine.

There are many ways to use writing as a therapeutic experience and it may lead to ideas and articles of your own. Give one of them a try.

Chapter Six

Focusing on the Home

Writing about the home can cover interior design, decorating, furniture, antiques and DIY projects. It also covers the garden, green ways of living, backyard farming, country living and keeping pets. There are a range of magazines and websites that fall into these subject areas, giving you, as a writer, even more opportunities to write lifestyle articles.

Inside and Outside

Magazines like Country Living or Better Homes and Gardens obviously do inside and outside - it's in their titles! But for other magazines, you will have to look at copies to see what they focus on more. Newspaper supplements and weekend sections are also worth looking at for writing opportunities. The Sunday Times (UK) has a Home section that looks at renovations, interiors, house prices and always includes a 'house of the week' feature. Check out your weekend newspapers to see what their supplements cover. Look at any local newspapers as well as national ones. There may be more opportunities with a newspaper closer to home.

Although many magazines carry articles on a little of both, there are also specific focus magazines. Period Living magazines covers just that! The World of Interiors has an inside focus. The English Garden focuses on - yes, you guessed it - English gardens!

An Easy Market?

It's not the easiest of writing genres to get into but there are certainly still possibilities. You will need to check out the magazines you would hope to write for to ascertain whether they take unsolicited manuscripts. Most of the house and home titles are high-end, glossy affairs and they tend not to accept unsolicited manuscripts sent in by freelancers. Find out the editor's or feature editor's name and send in your idea or proposal instead before you go ahead and write the full article.

Some magazines will ask for samples or cuttings of your work. If you have never written for this market before but really feel it is your forte, you can build up your portfolio in two ways. First, join up with websites where you can showcase your work. If you can start to build up an online presence, you can point editors towards your online articles. Second, consider having a blog. It's easy to set up a blog with online templates from websites such as Wordpress (www.wordpress.org). You can then regularly post short pieces of your writing as you update readers about house and home topics. Blogs are great for projects so say you are decorating your kitchen, you can write a daily blog about how you are progressing or if you are renovating an old home, a weekly blog can illuminate readers to the ups and downs of restoration. Again, this is another way of showing editors what you are capable of.

All about Interiors

When writing pieces about the interior of other people's houses, you will need two essential things - contacts and a decent camera. House and home magazines are glossy publications and they expect high quality photographs to go with their feature articles. There's no point in writing about how gorgeous the interior is of that old house up the road, if the readers can't see it.

When contacting a magazine with an idea, always tell the editor you can provide photographs. Then once the idea is accepted, check with them the quality and size of the photos that they need. Make sure that you use photo files that measure up to what the magazine requires and you'll receive payment for your article and your images.

Contacts are also important. You will need to get into people's houses to write up their histories and examine their furnishings. Some stately homes and grand houses belong to organisations that you can get in touch with for contact details. They sometimes have open weeks when they allow the general public to view their rooms or special evenings for pop-up restaurant meals or a special event that it might be in your interest to attend. Search the Internet for contact details to start off your contacts list. Once you start visiting houses and talking to the people that own them, they will give you further names and places of homes to write about.

Of course, if you live in a fantastic home or you have renovated or restored an old building yourself, you can write up your own experience. Editors like 'before' and 'after' articles where you can show the state of the house before it was worked on and the overall result when all the work was finished.

Writing about interiors also includes writing articles about the contents of homes like furniture, antiques, collectables, kitchen equipment and all the other essentials that kit out your home. As you know by now, I often write baby and parenting articles but I had an idea to mix the two. Hence this article published on the Vista website:

If you are expecting a baby, you will want to get your home ready for the arrival of your little one. Trips to the mall and superstores may leave you reeling from the many possibilities of baby furniture. There is so much choice out there but what do you really need?

The article goes through the main items of baby furniture that every mum will need plus how to cut costs and purchase furniture that has more than one purpose. You might not think that your area of writing is about the home but see how easy it is to adapt.

Decorating and DIY

How-to and instructional articles are a must in the decorating and DIY sections. Readers want tips and advice on how to create great rooms easily and, quite often, on a tight budget. Before you start writing any instructional or how-to article, check the skill level of the magazine's readers. Are the articles aimed at beginners or those with a certain knowledge level? Do you need to write from a very basic perspective or can you assume some prior knowledge and expertise?

Some instructional articles will need step-by-step pictures to go along with the text. This type of article is usually numbered 1-5 or 1-10. Each stage has a photo and explanation so readers can easily see how a project should progress. This is another type of article that you really have to try yourself and take the pictures as you go through the task, showing a complete, fantastic result at the end.

Health & Safety

Health and safety articles are used on home and house websites and cut across all different genres of magazine. If you have any knowledge of health and safety in the home, on the farm, or at work you might be able to supply them with good quality articles.

I've just sold an article on making your house safe for toddlers to a website which has a section on the home. You might think that's writing about the obvious but new mums will be anxious to prepare their homes and anxious grannies that have forgotten what it's like to have small children under foot will enjoy reading this kind of article. There is always a readership for health and safety articles. Think of who the piece is targeted at by checking out your magazine's readership and adopt the appropriate approach.

Homes Abroad

The British have a thing about France. There are several UK magazines about living in France, having a holiday home in France and renovating and repairing buildings in France. I'm sure there must be similar titles about Spain or the US but France and having a home in France seems to be a popular magazine subject.

This gives any writer the potential to look at a market for writing about homes that are not only in their own country but abroad too. If you have any experience of owning a holiday home or living in another country, you can use it for magazines that focus on living in any particular country.

Ongoing projects are popular articles but you do have to have been writing and taking photos of the project as it progressed. These can just be in note form that is then written up into a series of full-length articles at a later date. Humorous pieces are often used too as are readers' personal stories. Living in another country means a complete change of lifestyle and articles that focus on how you coped, what you did and how you did it are popular. These can include dealing with planning permissions, learning the language, finding the right foods to eat - everything that signals a new lifestyle and the experiences it brings.

Out in the Garden

House and home magazines often include garden sections from cooking outside, using the most of your space and purchasing and caring for outside furniture. They carry articles on garden plants, garden design, gardening techniques and practical projects. Some magazines are about gardens in general, others focus on vegetable growing or on organic growing.

Check out some of these gardening magazines:

All Year Garden (www.allyeargarden.com)
BBC Gardeners' World (www.gardenersworld.com)

Canadian Gardening (www.canadiangardening.com)

Garden Design (www.gardendesign.com)

Grower Talks (www.growertalks.com)

National Gardening (www.garden.org)

Organic Gardening (www.organicgardening.com)

Vegetable Gardener (www.vegetablegardener.com)

Green Living

My recent foray into writing for this genre was with an article about making your own wine. Whether you are a drinker or not, making your own wine is far healthier than shop-bought wine although ultimately, too much of any wine is not a good thing! I make my own wine using up the excess veg from the vegetable plot and also hedgerow flowers and berries. I've made allsorts - marigold, blackberry, carrot, rhubarb, pomegranate, black-currant - with a simple recipe passed down from my Nan and granddad who made wine during the Second World War. The article not only included the recipe but a step-by-step guide to making wine my way plus my reasons for doing so.

Many people want their environment, their home and their life to be healthier and green living magazines answer this need by providing alternatives, advice and information on how you can live a green life. The American magazine I wrote for - BackHome - has articles on gardening, having a green home, canning and pickling, and heating alternatives like stocking a wood pile or using solar energy.

Again projects are an important style of article for this kind of publication. If you have built a straw bale house, insulated your home with eco-friendly materials or installed an alternative heating system, you have material for an article. Or if you know someone else who lives a green lifestyle, you could always interview them for a feature that draws on their expertise.

Have you got Pets?

There are magazines for dog lovers, cat owners, fish keepers, bee keepers, hen breeders; if you keep any type of pet or farmyard animal, you can use your experiences to provide you with ideas for lifestyle articles. Cats, dogs and horses are the most popular pets that magazines focus on. The articles range from caring for your new pet to expert information on breeding and rearing your own. Advice on diets, exercise, healthcare and toys and equipment all feature in magazines that focus on animals.

Look up titles such as Cat World, I Love Cats, Animal Fair, Bird Times, Aquarium Fish, Reptiles, Dogs World Magazine and Modern Dog to give you an idea of the range of pet magazines that are out there. Then focus in on the type of animal that interest you most or that you have kept. What writing opportunities are there to share your experiences and inform other pet owners?

As well as domestic pets, there are a range of magazines that deal with country and farmyard animals. Country Smallholding is a popular UK magazine that accepts articles on looking after animals in a smallholding setting as well as other articles relevant to backyard farming. Their guidelines state that articles should be detailed and practical based on first-hand knowledge and experience. If you have lived or worked on a farm, writing lifestyle articles for this market could be right up your street.

Traditional Crafts Back in Fashion

Over the past few years, there has been more of a move back to traditional crafts, sustaining the ones we have or embracing them as a new skill or hobby. The recession has affected many people and there is a move back to making and mending things for ourselves. Magazine publishers have responded to this interest by bringing out magazines that give readers the low down on how to take up old crafts, giving them a new slant and a fresh perspective to entice another generation of readers.

Sewing, embroidery, patchwork quilting, beading, paper-crafting and knitting are covered in magazines specifically catering to people interested in these crafts. Editors of these magazines constantly need well thought out new ideas for projects and things to make. If you are good at craftwork and can provide supporting pictures, these magazines may provide successful markets for you.

Don't forget green living and country living magazines. They also cover crafts and the different ways of using them in our lives today. For more information on writing for the country market, check out Suzanne Ruthven's book, The Country Writers' Craft: how to write for the country, regional and rural markets.

The Vintage Scene

There is a recent trend in all things vintage and new magazines have sprung up to cover this kind of lifestyle. You may not think of vintage as being a lifestyle choice but many people combine their love of the 50s with the clothes they wear, the cars they drive and the houses they decorate. And it's not just the 50s, I'm not sure of the exact dates that make something vintage but whatever era you love, it can become a part of your lifestyle.

One magazine, Vintage Life (www.vintagelifemagazine.com), covers style and fashion, hair and beauty, house and home, music and film; focusing on everything great about the 20s, 30s, 40s, 50s, 60s through to the 70s - all in one magazine. And there are others out there to try with your lifestyle articles. On a quick Google search, I found Pretty Nostalgic, Vintage Lifestyle and Simply Vintage magazines. If you live a vintage lifestyle then why not write about it?

Choosing an Area to Focus on

Are you an innie or an outie?! Are you more interested in your home than you are your garden? Or happier being outside rather than in? If you have a preference, then you should focus your writing on what appeals to you most.

Does the thought of decorating get you rushing to your nearest supply store or hiding under the duvet pretending it will be alright for another year? Would you rather cuddle up to a pet than attend a vintage car rally?

Think about what your strengths are in regard to writing about all things house, garden and lifestyle.

Try this Exercise: The 5Ws

We have looked at lots of possibilities for lifestyle articles; interiors, gardens, decorating, crafts, homes abroad and the vintage scene included. Let's now try and drum up an idea for an article using the 5Ws - what, who, where, when and why - plus how. How becomes more important with home articles as you may need to explain in-depth how something was achieved. Take a piece of paper or grab that notebook and list the 5Ws. I've come up with:

What: buying a house
Who: that would be me!
Where: in France
When: approx. 7 years ago
Why: I keep asking myself this but I think I had an idea about renovating an old barn to become a writer's retreat!
How: by visiting holiday home shows, going over to France, talking to estate agents and then going through the legal process

There's a wealth of material I could use to write up this article and send it to an editor. How did you get on? Have you got the basis for another lifestyle article now? If so, get writing!

Chapter Seven

Writing about Food & Fashion

Food and fashion are some people's absolute passions. They are two areas of writing that have received an increasing focus over recent years. You can even study food and fashion journalism at degree level now, which shows you how well trained specific writers are in their craft.

Looking at Food and Eating it

This is one area of writing when going to market can actually mean going to market! Visits to local farmers produce stalls or pop up French markets can provide you with ideas and give you a chance to sample foods that you may not have tasted before. Being a food writer is all about using your sense of taste. If you are squeamish about trying out new foods or prefer to stick to a strict diet, then food writing is not going to be your genre. You will need to be able to use new ingredients, taste strange delicacies and fine-tune your taste buds so that you can tell the difference between low and high quality foods.

Food writing, like writing about interiors, is a specialist subject. Look at the names of writers of food articles in the Sunday newspapers. You will probably have heard of them, seen their work before and recognise their style of writing. That's not to say that you cannot break into this market but you are going to have to do some work.

With any area of writing that requires expert knowledge or expertise, you need to build a portfolio. We have discussed before about having your own blog or using social media to promote your work. This is especially the case with food writing - if you can regularly blog new recipes or have a website that focuses on a particular area of food-writing, you will build up an online portfolio.

A friend of mine who writes cookery articles says you need to find your niche and then promote it. Pick a certain type of cookery and use it to build up your credibility as a writer. You can branch out when you have a portfolio to your name. So it could be desserts, Indian food, vegan cookery or cupcakes - whatever your foodie interest, stick with it while you are starting to write.

Different Diets

I mentioned vegan cookery above and then there is gluten-free, vegetarian, kosher, lactose-intolerant, salt-free... there are many diet preferences that people take for health reasons, moral reasons or just because their doctor told them so! Be conscious of who you are writing for. If you have a particular diet yourself, consider writing for magazines that target this readership and draw on your own experiences. General health magazines, women's magazines and family focused magazines might be interested in diet articles as well as the actual food magazines.

I wrote an article about bringing up your children to a vegetarian lifestyle. It started like this:

'If you are vegetarian or considering becoming one, you are by no means alone. There are four million vegetarians in the UK, 12 per cent of which are veggie kids under the age of sixteen...There are several reasons why you might want to choose an alternative diet for your baby. You might be veggie yourself, on moral or health grounds. You might wish to change the whole family's diet to one free of health scares. Or you may find that your baby dislikes meat. It doesn't matter why you opt for a vegetarian diet for your baby. Bringing up your child this way is a positively healthy decision...'
(Your New Baby, 2001).

It went on to include the key vitamins that vegetarians need to ensure are in their diets, what baby food you can make that contain sufficient dietary elements and where to find further information.

A Few Ideas

Mums and Nans can be great sources for recipe ideas. Women in years past created family cookbooks and many of these have been raided to provide new recipe ideas for today's readers. Some of the best nostalgic recipes have come from a writer's own family. You might have to change around some of the ingredients and update their use. My Nan ate whale blubber in the Second World War and I don't think anyone would want to read about that recipe now!

Seasonal recipes are always a hit but you have to think outside of the box. An English traditional Christmas meal of turkey and stuffing has been done to death so what other alternatives are there? What do people eat around the globe? What can a vegan or vegetarian eat for an interesting Christmas meal? Think of readers who don't eat the traditional meals and see if you can come up with some exciting recipes for them.

Students are always looking for low budget meals and I'm not just talking beans on toast. Great ideas that are simple and cheap to make but provide a nutritional meal are always sought after. Dinners on a shoestring are always popular as well as articles on cutting down your food shopping weekly spend.

Quick and easy recipes are a good idea for busy mums, people who work long hours or people like me that can only be bothered to cook in rapid time. When I'm looking at new recipes, I'm put off by long lists of ingredients. I don't want a never-ending list to take around the supermarket with me. Recipes with only three or four ingredients are intriguing. Will the meal actually taste good with so little in it? Everyone is different and although many people want quick and easy meals, there are others who love nothing more than to spend a day baking.

Check out your market, whether it's a magazine, newspaper or website, to see how complicated the recipes get or whether they prefer simple and easy recipes.

Writing up Recipes

What's the next best thing to eating food - writing about it! But writing a recipe has to be absolutely clear and well-thought out or your readers will end up in a mess. Recipes are separated into two parts; the ingredients list and the method or preparation. Ingredients should be listed in the order of use and all amounts should be correct and consistent. Write out the measurements in grams and ounces or if sticking to one type of measurement, make sure it is the same throughout. Check and double-check your amounts. The only way of doing this is, of course, to cook up your recipe and that way you will know exactly how much of each ingredient you will need.

When writing up the preparation section, break it into steps. Include the equipment you will need. So you might write *'place the flour into a large bowl'* or *'in a pestle and mortar, crush garlic, parsley and black pepper.'* Remember to include all cooking times and temperatures. Don't overcomplicate your instructions. Write short sentences that are clear and concise. Alert your readers to any problems that might arise like opening the oven door too soon or over-cooking. End your recipe with serving instructions or storage details as appropriate.

Always try out recipes before unleashing them on the reading public. How do you know that it tastes great or only takes 20 minutes to prepare and cook unless you have tried it?

Cookery for Kids

Two options here; easy recipes for kids to cook and meals for kids like packed lunches or dinners that hide the veg. I talked about writing cookery articles for kids in a previous chapter on writing parenting and childcare articles. Refer back to that if your creative juices are leading you in that direction.

Also think about what meals have worked for your children or grandchildren. Healthy school lunches are an obvious choice. Parents of fussy eaters might need ideas for recipes that hide foods they don't like. Ideas for snacks and afterschool nibbles are also popular.

Holiday Experiences

People tend to try new foods when they are on holiday. Local cuisine can introduce you to new ingredients and new ways of cooking. I remember travelling in Spain and seeing roadside sellers making huge pans of paella on cast iron gas rings and when I went to Africa, fish being barbequed ready to eat straight from market stalls. Holidays have a lot of potential for food writers. Take notes the next time you are away and never be afraid to ask a chef or cook what their ingredients are or to ask for their recipe. Some will not want to give away family secrets but if you explain you are a writer and would like to send their recipe for an exquisite meal to a magazine for publication, they may just give you the information you need.

If you really want to follow the route of a food writer, you can also base your next holiday around food. Take a cookery class in Tuscany or learn to make gourmet food in Paris. Open yourself up to cooking experiences in other countries and you will have the basis for many foodie articles.

Kitchen Tips

A quick and easy way to start building up your portfolio as a food writer is to provide kitchen tips. Many women's magazines as well as food magazines encourage readers to send in their tips and advice. Sometimes these are accompanied by a small photo but they could just be a few lines of text that explain a way to make savings, swop ingredients, store food or bake to perfection. Think of the little ways in which you make cooking easier, steal ideas from your mum or grandparents, and write them up in a short and sweet few lines to send into kitchen tips pages.

Reviewing Restaurants

Free food I hear you cry! Sorry, unless you're a top reviewer for a top magazine or newspaper, you won't be offered a budget for dining out every night. However, when you do eat out, you could consider writing up your experience as a review. There are many new writers that post their reviews on websites and again, this can add to a body of work to show editors.

When writing any type of review, look for the pluses and minuses. A review should give some balance and reasoning to why it was a good or bad eating experience. Some editors use rating systems so you might need to grade a restaurant's service, food, wine or ambience. Remember always that a reader could decide whether to visit a restaurant or not based on your recommendation. Reviews can really make or break restaurants so be sure of your facts and certain of your viewpoint before you write up a review.

Don't forget to include details such as address, telephone number, whether you need to book and the average prices of food and wine. Mention any special deals or set menus, including which nights these are offered.

What about Fashion?

Fashion is big business and so are the glossy magazines that cover the latest in fashion trends, clothing lines, fashion shows and the newest beauty products. Magazines like Vogue, In Style, Elle, Allure, Glamour, and Harper's Bazaar cover the world of fashion but every magazine is different and as with any market, it is advisable to look at the different types of fashion magazine to see where your style would fit.

Unfortunately, fashion is one of the hardest markets to break into but, as we have said before, if you build up a portfolio by writing for smaller, perhaps regional magazines or by blogging on a website, you can build up your readership and have something to show editors.

A lot of these magazines don't use freelance writers but have their own in-house staff. If you really want to get into this line of work, start adding to a portfolio but also look around for internships or vacancies where you can get a foot in the door.

Choosing a focus is advisable. If you can concentrate on an area of fashion like vintage, men's or kids' or focus on hair, natural beauty or accessories, you have more chance of being seen as an expert in that area of writing.

Then when you are ready to contact an editor, do so with a query and attach your biography and links to any online articles or blogs. Check out any writers' guidelines beforehand and do your market research, then at least you will have covered all your bases and acted professionally. They may not send you out to cover a fashion show in Milan but you may get the opportunity to start with smaller articles.

Keeping up with the Trends

Fashion is all about knowing what is in and what the next trends will be. This means keeping ahead of what is happening in the fashion world by attending shows and events and keeping a close eye out for new ranges and up-and-coming designers.

Fashion is a global fascination and top shows are held in Paris, London, Milan and New York. Subscribe to websites with news feeds about celebrities and fashion so that you know when there is a major event coming up and even if you can't attend, you will be aware of what was showcased there and what the fashion predictions are for the next six months to a year.

Read the type of magazine that you would like to write for so that you build up knowledge of what they have covered and you have an idea of what they cover when. Fashion is seasonal and magazines will concentrate on winter clothing, holiday wear, ski fashions and party clothes at different times of the year. Keep a fashion calendar, working at least six months in advance so that you know when to write about seasonal pieces.

Beautiful You

Make-up, hair, beauty products and jewellery all add to our appearance and make an appearance in fashion magazines as well as mags that specifically focus on beauty. Beauty articles can range from dealing with problem skin to make-up tips for a night on the town. Hair articles cover the latest trends, how the celebs are styling their hair and the newest products to hit the shelves.

If you are interested in writing this type of article, look up the writers' guidelines for the magazine you hope to write for or look for beauty sites online that take freelance articles. Many of these articles are highly photographic; they include pictures of models, close-up shots of styled hair or made-up lips and eyes. That's why a lot of these articles are written in-house because they also have to have the photos to go with the text and there are often far more images than there is writing. However, I have seen really good advice and photos displayed on web pages that take a reader through their make-over or new hairstyle step by step. You will find more opportunities to use your writing and photo-graphic skills on the web especially as you build up your expertise.

Style Tips and Advice

How-to articles, tips, and practical advice are probably the most sought-after articles from freelancers. This type of article can easily be slotted into other types of magazines so it widens your opportunities to break into the fashion market. Think of things like how to dress to hide your pregnancy bump or how to buy the best baby clothes on a budget - ways in which readers can get an idea that could help them out.

Try this Exercise: The How-to Article

Pick one topic; hair, make-up or style. Make a list of at least ten titles for articles. Don't think about it too much. Just freeflow your ideas and jot them down, no matter how good or bad they sound at the time. If you get stuck, think of what readership an article could be targeted to; students, new mums, teenagers, older women, scruffy men! Start each title with *'How to ...'*. When you've managed ten, go back and circle your best three ideas. Now pick your top one and write a how-to article of around 500 words.

Writing for Teens

Don't forget the teen fashion market. Yes, you will need to be aware of what teenage girls see as fashion and what trends they are currently following but there is an opportunity here to write how-to articles and beauty basics for a younger readership. Grab a handful of these magazines the next time you are out shopping or browse a few teen style websites. Better still, talk to teenagers to see what info they'd love to read about and what they really want to know.

When looking for magazines, check out:

Seventeen (www.seventeen.com)
CosmoGIRL! (www.cosmogirl.com)
Bliss (www.mybliss.co.uk)
Shout (www.shoutmag.co.uk)

Reviewing Beauty Products

One way of starting out in fashion and beauty writing is to get yourself on review panels. Scan magazine pages for the possibility of doing a reader's review. Women's magazines often have panels of testers that try out a product, write a short review on it and give it a rating. You could also check out market research companies to see if they need product testers. That way you will have advance knowledge of a new product coming out on the market and will be able to write about it before anyone else does!

Chapter Eight

From Cars to Computing

Now we're getting technical! Writing about cars, motorbikes, boys' toys and computers does require some knowledge but these markets are always looking for writers. Many of the magazines accept freelance work, especially those that detail projects and can provide photographic images to go with them. If you are interested in writing about cars and other forms of transport, you have a good chance of seeing your work in print.

Trains, Planes and Automobiles

Let's not forget motorbikes, tractors, classic cars, trucks, retro models, buses, Landrovers... if transport is your passion, there are plenty of markets that need your specialist knowledge and enthusiasm. And it's not just the actual vehicles, boats or planes that are written about, it's the whole lifestyle that surrounds them. Many train enthusiasts collect models, classic car nuts attend meets and auctions, plane buffs go to watch aerial displays and may be interested in military planes and history as well. There are a range of article opportunities for any writer who loves their transport.

Just take a look at any one of this type of magazine. My husband loves Landrovers and in each edition there are articles about buying them, maintaining them and improving them. There are articles about restoration, typical faults and fixes, places to drive them, shows, events, historical pieces, new products and all the accessories you need. Yes, some of these articles are technical and would need an expert to write them but others share stories of trips made, projects undertaken and the current marketplace for buying and selling.

Car Enthusiasts needed

I have worked for a few different content providers and I have noticed that some of them always have car assignments for freelance writers. It seems to me that car enthusiasts are needed for articles like *the top five best family cars, the best car for town-driving* and *the latest eco models.* Articles that update readers on the latest models and compare their value and performance are used regularly.

The only two articles I have ever written that involved cars was one on child safety that looked at what type of seat to use and how to buy a petrol remote controlled car. Both were for websites. Check out websites like Textbroker (www.text broker.com or www.textbroker.co.uk), Wisegeek (www.wise geek.com) and About (www.about.com) to see what opportunities they present to transport loving writers.

There also seem to be many more opportunities in print magazines and if you can provide photos as well, the pay is good. It's definitely an area worth getting into if you are a car (or other transport) enthusiast.

Try this Exercise: My First Car

Think you might be interested in writing for this genre? Now depending on how old you are will determine whether we are talking classics or not! Either way, what was your first car or bike? Do you still have it or have photos of it? Do some research on your first car or bike and find out its history. Was it from a major manufacturer or a more select company? Where were they based and are they still producing new models? Try writing a nostalgic piece based around your first vehicle but with added information on the history of the manufacturer and their models to date.

Check out the Market

Excited already? Want to make some money writing for car and bike magazines? Take a look at these markets, all of which take freelance articles:

Automobile Quarterly (www.autoquarterly.com) are looking for technical articles, photo features, biographies and historical articles.

Auto Restorer (www.autorestorermagazine.com) want auto restoration pieces, how-to's, photo features and product news.

Classic Trucks (www.classictrucks.com) need technical articles, how-to's, new product reviews and travel pieces.

Friction Zone (www.friction-zone.com) is a motorcycle magazine that uses non-fiction articles, column pieces, fillers and even some fiction.

Autocar (www.autocar.co.uk) welcome news stories, features, interviews and ideas.

Classic Bike (www.classicbike.co.uk) is looking for industry stories, how-to's, features and news.

The Vintage Scene

Vintage strikes again! Many people love to look back into the past and recreate and renovate classical living. We saw that fashion is one area where a love of vintage can give you ideas for lifestyle writing. Vintage transport is another such area but one that perhaps has far more opportunities to see your work in print. The vintage car scene has many avid followers and magazines and websites encourage readers to send in their articles on how they have restored a vehicle. Steam train enthusiasts, classic bike and vintage tractor fans also have their own magazines. It's not just about the vehicles but about the lifestyle as well.

Specialist Hobby Magazines

Modified cars, hot-rods, radio-controlled cars, classic toy trains, fine-scale models and kit planes are all included under the category of specialist hobby magazines. Again, a lot of the articles used here are the project type that follow a restoration or a build. They also weigh in with a lot of technical information and really go into detail for the hobby enthusiast who isn't afraid of getting their hands dirty.

If your love of transport has put you in touch with one of these hobbies then think about using your knowledge to write technical and how-to articles for these markets. Most specialist magazines accept articles from freelancers and are always willing to look at ideas for new features.

Writing about Boys Toys and Gadgets

I'm not being sexist by suggesting there are boys' toys! Of course, girls enjoy toys and gadgets too. Every year in Dublin, there is a boys' toys event that showcases the latest gadgets and grown-up entertainment thingummys. What I'm referring to is the market for things like remote-controlled helicopters, underwater cameras, mini bikes, robots, phones, go-karts, camcorders - helpful stuff, silly stuff and technological stuff. This area of writing is popular with bloggers and is also the subject of many a product review.

Product Reviewing

You can find opportunities to review products by applying for reader's panel positions or becoming a tester, but you can also send in ideas and suggestions for product reviews to editors. Give brief details of the overall category and how many products you expect to review, so for instance, *tablet devices - the top five sellers* or *desktop PCs - from budget to high performance.* These examples have been done before so stick your thinking cap on and, if you can come up with great ideas for product reviews, get your ideas in to the relevant editors of the magazines you'd like to write for.

You can also add reviews to any blog or website that you have. One way of doing this is to contact companies directly and give them the details of your site or blog whilst asking for samples. You won't be sent the latest Ipod or new model of car but you will start building up your portfolio and could get fresh on the market information as well as smaller samples like game demos or test versions of new apps.

Writing about Computers

There are several computing publications which could prove a profitable market for lifestyle writers if you are interested in this subject. PC Format (www.pcformat.co.uk) covers performance hardware and gaming, Computeractive (www.computer active.co.uk) uses consumer and computer technology articles, Computing (www.computing.co.uk) is a newspaper for IT professionals and Smart Computing (www.smartcomputing .com) is on the look-out for how-to articles, new product reviews and technical pieces.

And then there's the blog. I know I have mentioned blogging now in a few places and you may or may not be a computer fan but if you're going to be writing about computers, what better way than to share your knowledge online. Just be aware of who you are targeting as your readership. Is it the complete beginner, the somewhat knowledgeable or the tech expert? Decide at which level you can write about computers and computing and pitch your writing to that type of reader.

Try this Exercise: Check your Level

Imagine that a friend of yours has just bought a new PC and they want to know the best ways of keeping their new computer running smoothly. You could suggest things like installing good anti-virus software or using disk clean-up and disk defragmenter functions. Write a 500 word article based on what you know. Then give it to someone else to read. Try giving it to someone you know who hasn't much knowledge of computers and another person who uses them all the time. Who does the article appeal to most? How easy is your style of writing to follow? Use this exercise to help you decide what level of reader knowledge to pitch your articles at.

Getting Technical

How much of an expert do you need to be? Well, you definitely have to know what you are talking about. I wrote a lot about writing for the Internet in my previous book, *The Writer's Internet*. I could say I know a lot about computers on the basis of that but I know I don't. Of course, I know enough about how writers can use the Internet and write for the Internet but I know next to nothing about programming, software development or the technical side of things.

But that's just me. Avid computer users will have expert knowledge and skills that they can draw on to write the more technical articles. When contacting editors, it would be ideal if you also had qualifications in some type of computing to back up your technical expertise.

Or you could just stick with basic knowledge articles aimed at a readership that hasn't been brought up with computers and technology like the over 60s or you could target a different type of reader with computing articles.

I once wrote a piece entitled *It's Never too Early to Learn* aimed at the parents of small children. The skill level was basic but encouraged parents to help their children pick up the skills they will need.

'Computers are everywhere these days. Whether you are testing your car, booking a holiday or paying the bills, you can bet a computer has some part in it. Children today will grow up in a world where computers are commonplace, whether we like it or not... You might already have a computer at home or you might be considering

buying one. Even if you do not have the funds but still want your child to feel comfortable with computers, there are ways in which to introduce your child to the technological age. It's never too early to introduce your child to a piece of equipment that will feature largely in their school days and working lives.' (Your New Baby, 2002).

Gaming

Where there are computers, there is gaming! Ok so people also play games on the Xbox, Playstation or other types of games consoles but gaming is big business. Again, reviews are used to help readers decide what games are best for them as well as reviews of gaming accessories like steering wheels, chairs and control pads.

Send in your ideas or queries to magazines such as Game Informer (www.gameinformer.com), PC Gamer (www.pcgamer .com) or the official magazine for the console you love to play and want to write about!

Chapter Nine

Writing for the Travel Market

Lifestyle writing includes writing about travel. From far-flung destination to hotel reviews and day trips out, travel writing lets readers know details about where to go and what to do. It doesn't mean that you have to be a world-wide traveller, you can write about places in your own country or specialise in things to do in your own area.

What Destination?

Open any travel magazine and you will see articles about far-flung destinations like Bali, Iceland and Tibet. These destinations make great articles but you have to have the money to travel there and investigate more than what the average tourist sees. Many people go on holiday to hotel complexes where they take a few trips out, sun bathe and take a dip in the pool. Travel writing has got to contain more than that and, as a travel writer, it means when you go abroad you have to immerse yourself in the history, culture and customs of that country.

If you eat in the hotel restaurant every night, watch the cabaret in the hotel bar and only visit water parks and tourist beaches, your writing is not going to say a lot about the country you are visiting. You need to delve deep. Eat in the restaurants that are popular to the inhabitants, see the places that have historical significance and really get out and about to the places that are not so frequented by tourists to really give a good view of what is so special and so enjoyable about travelling around that country or destination.

As a new travel writer, you won't be given free holidays so whenever you go on your own holidays, you need to be taking notes and keeping a journal of people you met, places you visited and any background information you find out. You can do more research when you get home but while you are there you have to act and think like a writer and open yourself up to the travel experience. Of course, you can still have a few days by the pool but your article is not going to focus on that, so make diligent notes and take amazing photos while you are there and you are surrounded by all that country has to offer.

Travel with a Purpose

Fund-raising trips, community projects and travel with a purpose are also covered in travel magazines and travel sections. Do you know someone that is going to help build a school in Africa or is travelling to a natural disaster area to help out? This type of article can be really topical and also drum up support or funds for the project and people it highlights. It needs to be timed so that the idea is in to an editor well before the trip has started as it could lead to several articles, before and after the trip.

When I travelled to Africa as part of the Tanzanian Gender Networking Programme, I wrote an article before we left that built on the reasons for the exchange, who was going and why. Then on my return I wrote several articles including attending the Gender Networking Festival and visiting Kivulini's Women's Rights organisation.

'Travelling to the North of Tanzania, Dar es Salaam and Zanzibar meant a hectic trip with 8 flights over 13 days but it truly gave an eye opening view of the struggles African women face, the society they are hoping to change and the transformation that has already begun through the hard work of the African feminist movement' (Changing Ireland, 2007).

Is there a group of volunteers heading across the globe from your locality? Do you know someone who has been involved in community projects or do you participate in such trips yourself? This type of travel article is steeped in the culture and customs of another country and brings into focus issues that people are facing around the world. Is it something you could write about?

Specialist Holidays

There are several markets for travel writing about specialist holidays. Think about the different holidays that you could take that have a theme. There are history holidays, cooking holidays, wine-tasting trips, cycling adventures, walking holidays, writer's retreats, spa breaks - all these get covered in travel magazines and magazines that focus on specific topics. If you don't have the budget to travel at the moment, look to see what kind of specialist holidays are available in your area. I live close to the sea so there are things like surfing, horse-riding and horse-drawn carriage holidays in my locality. Is there something around where you live or something where you have travelled before that would make a good article?

What are your hobbies? If you enjoy things like golfing, surfing or snowboarding, look at the magazines you read to see if they have a travel section. That way when you take your next trip, you can combine your likes with travel and come up with articles that cover both.

Closer to Home

You can still be a travel writer even if you don't go abroad three times a year. It doesn't matter where you live in the world, you can write a travel article about it. You may be so used to where you live that you don't see it through a traveller's eyes so remember to look at your town or a local resort from a fresh perspective. What would people do if they came to stay there on holiday? What activities could they take part in? Are there festivals or events that it would be exciting to attend?

If you live in a city, what is the best time of year to stay? What is there to see and do? There may be opportunities to write up walking tours that take in historic sites, or you could write an article on the museums or art galleries that people could visit.

Visit the hotels, holiday homes or apartments that are let out to tourists. Do they have the potential to be included in an article? You might be able to review local tourist accommodation for a travel website and start building up your travel writing portfolio.

Holidays with a Difference

You might be the kind of person that has made an incredible voyage or you might have gone on a journey that is out of the ordinary - or you are planning to. I spent three months travelling Europe in a Land Rover when my children were small and I kept a daily diary so that I could write up the experience when we got home. I sold our story as a two-part travel feature to Motorcaravan Motorhome Monthly along with several images of the trip. It began:

'An idea germinated one cold winter night in the wilderness of Co. Leitrim. It formed, spurred on by the longing for warmer climates and European culture. The idea was a journey, by Land Rover, to Portugal, investigating France and Spain, en route.'

And continued to tell the tale of our journey interspersed with stories of who we met and where we stayed. *'Heading on to Carnac, we stopped for several days by the river, sampling the delights on offer in this brandy-producing region. Continuing on to Pau, the gateway to the Pyrenees, we drove for six to eight hours a day. A stop at Montguyon provided an interesting break. A disused garage was home to a 1940s truck graveyard. Monsieur Legendre, the proprietor, couldn't believe our interest in them. He suggested we took them home with us. A future restoration project, perhaps?'* (Motorcaravan Motorhome Monthly, 2000).

If you are undertaking an unusual trip or journey, keep accurate notes or a diary as your adventure progresses so that you can write it up when you get home. On the other hand, if you know someone else that is going on a holiday with a difference or on a fund-raising trek, talk to them about helping them to write up their journey on their return. You might find the opportunity to ghost write an article for them or report on their adventures.

Days Out

Your articles don't have to be about week-long holidays or a fortnight in the sun, you can also write about days out. These are especially used when there are school holidays due and parents are looking for things to do with their kids, but you could also cover days out from a different perspective. What about a romantic day out? Or what about a thrill-seeking day out including bungee jumping or a parachute jump?

Reviewing Hotels

Many magazines take hotel reviews but there are also lots of websites that you can add your hotel review to like Trip Advisor (www.tripadvisor.com), Holidays Uncovered (www.holidays-uncovered.co.uk), Holiday Watchdog (www.holidaywatchdog.com) and Hotel Chatter (www.hotelchatter.com).

Look at the structure of previous reviews before you submit your own. Is there a rating system? What is covered in the review - service, cleanliness, eating, amenities?

Finding your Niche

With travel writing, you may find that you would like to concentrate on a particular area of travel. It could be that a country speaks to you more than others. Do you love France? Could you write about city breaks to Paris and Lyon and where to go camping for an authentic French experience? Perhaps Spain calls to you - you could write about the food, the culture and the best places to stay on a budget. If you have really fallen in love with a country when you have visited it and you intend to travel there more, then consider focusing on that country as your travel niche.

Be aware of who your audience is. Are you more comfortable writing for the armchair traveller or the adventurer? Look at the difference between these types of travel magazines. You might find that you what to write for a particular audience like young people, older people, gay travellers or for those who have disabilities.

Travel articles also come in a few different types. There is the first person experience article that literally tells readers about a holiday you had. There are humorous pieces that are usually used to make fun about negative or frustrating experiences. You will also find straight-forward features, best ofs, top tens and comparison articles.

Try this Exercise: The Holiday from Hell

I'm pretty sure that everyone has a holiday horror story. We always hope that our holidays will be a nice pleasant break that will leave us refreshed and invigorated but that's not always the case. At the end of the trip I made to Europe that I mentioned earlier our Land Rover broke down. We were on the way to the ferry and had no money left. The Land Rover was stocked with food but it was taken away by a breakdown truck. Our insurance company put us up in a hotel and hired a taxi to take us to the ferry port the next morning. We were tired and hungry and we had no money for food. It was late so we just all fell asleep but the next morning the taxi driver took pity on us and bought us breakfast. We didn't get the Land Rover back for two weeks and you know all that food that was in it? Yep, absolutely rotten!

So, that's my tale but what is yours? Think of a time when your holiday, day trip out or city break didn't go according to plan. Write it up as either a straight-forward holiday from hell story or inject some humour into it. Try writing about 800 words - the average length of one page article - and send it in to a travel magazine of your choice.

Finding a Market

There are lots of travel magazines on the market, some of which are listed next, but don't forget magazines that cater for other topics. Say you've taken a golfing holiday, the magazines for golfers will be interested in looking at your article or food magazines could be interested in a trip you made to a cookery school. Don't forget to check out magazines and newspapers that have a monthly or weekly travel section that you could add to. Travel writing opportunities are everywhere - start looking out for them.

Have a look at:

Conde Nast Traveller (www.cntraveller.com)
Good Holiday Magazine (www.goodholidayideas.com)
Motorcaravan Motorhome Monthly
   (www.outandaboutlive.co.uk)
Practical Caravan (www.practicalcaravan.com)
Camping Today (www.fcrv.org)
International Living (www.internationalliving.com)
Islands (www.islands.com)
Spa Life (www.spalifemagazine.com)
Travel and Leisure (www.travelandleisure.com)
Travel Naturally (www.internaturally.com)
Verge (www.vergemagazine.org)

Writing the Travel article

This is one type of article where you really have to bring your description to life. Readers want to feel that they are there, in the same surroundings you have been. It's a case of showing and not telling - the age old writer's maxim. Write a description that sets the scene and really brings the country or place to life. That means using the five senses to their full effect when you talk about meeting people, visiting places and staying in vivid locations.

Try to avoid clichés. *The sun was hot and the sea was blue.* Yes, we know, been there, done that - it doesn't tell a reader anything different. Describe what is unusual, extraordinary and exciting about the place. Even if it was dull, boring and the most awful place you have ever visited, tell your readers that but use new words to bring your writing to life. Dig out a thesaurus and look for other ways of saying the same thing. Editors really don't want to publish travel articles that sound like they have been written again and again.

And while we're talking about editors - use a catchy title to grasp their attention. Things like *A Day in Paris* or *The Best Hotel in Crete* just won't do. You need to think of better ways to title your article. Play around with words. Use something that will hook your reader (and editor!) in and excite them to want to read further.

Using Photos

The other thing that is really important about travel articles is the photos that go with them. The good news for you is that you will get paid for both - your article and your photos. The bad news is... well, there is no bad news unless you forget to take them! Just remember to take lots of shots of the various things that might illustrate your article. Today with digital cameras this shouldn't be a problem. If you're worried about your camera being stolen or damaged while you are away, email them to yourself or store them on a cloud server to be accessed on your return.

I remember sending in print photos with articles and having to number them and send them in with an accompanying list of captions. Nowadays, editors prefer to be emailed files that they can browse through and select the best images that suit their publication. Check the photo guidelines for the magazine or website you are sending your work to for details on how they want your photographs submitted. Make sure you are sending in the correct file type and size.

When you are taking your photos, do so from different angles so that an editor has the choice of shots. A straight-on view of the Eiffel Tower or Big Ben shows nothing different and has been used many times before but if you can take the shot from high up, across the river, or used as a backdrop, you might come up with something new. You might like to take a course in digital photography or read up on useful techniques to give you more skills but you don't need to be an expert - not at this stage, anyway. I'm no photographer but I have managed to sell several photos alongside articles of all descriptions.

Doing your Research

If you are going to write about travel, guess what? You have to travel! But you also will need to undertake some research before you go and use it to help you write your article when you get back. Before undertaking any trip, do as much reading up, googling and reading of reviews as you can do. Opt for guidebooks like the Rough Guide and Lonely Planet series that give details of where you are going plus extras. Read books by other lifestyle and non-fiction writers about the place you are about to visit. See what they had to say about the place so you know what has been written about it before. Talk to others who have been. This is one of the best ways to find out info that doesn't appear in all the books. When my kids were young we stayed in a hotel in Crete. It was right at the end of the tourist strip which wouldn't be a usual place we'd head for, but a friend of ours had told us that that hotel was great because just behind it you could walk into real Crete, full of winding roads and little roadside cafes. It was a great base for us that we could use to explore the interior of the island from and we wouldn't have found it without the advice of a friend.

Without sounding too rigid, try and plan your itinerary or schedule so that you cover the main places you want to visit but be open to following new leads. Always stop in at local museums or tourist centres to find out other places of interest as well as background information.

When you are away, pick up all the leaflets and brochures you can carry. Save tickets, timetables and receipts. This may sound excessive but I have often forgotten to note something exactly in my notebook but have then found the details on a piece of paper that I carried home with me. They can act as memory prompts as well as providing you with facts you have forgotten.

Chapter Ten

The Over 50s Lifestyle

In recent years, more magazines have come onto the market that concentrate on lifestyle and living for the over 50s. Their focus is especially for people who perhaps may have grown-up families, have retired, have more disposable income and are looking to make the most of their lives regardless of aging and the health problems it may bring. The attitude of the over 50s market is upbeat and positive and it could provide you with many opportunities for lifestyle writing with a particular readership in mind.

What's Different about this Market?

The over 50s market is definitely more magazine based although there are some websites that take lifestyle articles for this age range. You might find these magazines categorised as 'senior' or 'retirement' but whatever way they are labelled, they are geared to an older readership that are in the later years of their lives.

For example, Yours (www.yours.co.uk) is a British magazine for the over-50s that has both a print version and a web version. They say that they cater to a friendly community where readers can share stories and laughter and find all kinds of advice on topics that matter including health, beauty, travel, fashion, finance and consumer issues. They also have articles about the stars of yesterday and the way we used to live.

The US magazine, AARP (www.aarp.org), makes a point of saying that their editorial content enhances the quality of life for all by promoting independence, dignity and purpose. Yes, the readership might be older but we're not talking bed pans and aching joints here. All magazines for the over 50s look at aging as a part of life, offering encouraging, constructive and affirmational articles.

Over 50s magazines tend to have more columns for readers to send their stories into and humour quite often features in these. Mature Living (www.lifeway.com) has a Cracker Barrel column for humorous quips and verses, a Grandparents Brag Board for humorous stories about what grand-kids and great grand-kids get up to as well as gardening, crafts, food and inspirational columns. Mature Years (www.matureyears.com) has a Merry-go-round column for cartoons, jokes and humorous verse plus finance, health and inspirational columns. And all of these columns are open to freelance lifestyle writers to send in their writing.

You will need to look at some copies of this type of magazine to see how different they are than those for the younger generations. Pay particular attention to house style and the topics covered before submitting your ideas and articles.

Important Topics for the over 50s

The topics that are covered in this type of lifestyle magazine are not so different from magazines that are aimed at a younger readership but they have a different slant or point of view. Take finances for example, where younger readers might be interested in budgeting, mortgages and buying their first home, an older readership is more interested in what to do with their savings, whether they can afford a holiday home and the best ways to pass on their investments to their kids.

Health, of course, is a huge factor but no doom and gloom please! Informative, practical and supportive articles are what's needed here. Food, dining out, travel, beauty and fashion are still just as important but from an older perspective.

So you want to write a beauty article? Look at products for mature skin, find out what the best beauty regime is for older women and talk to the more mature lady for her advice and tips. If you're not over 50 yourself, then you will need to talk to people who are to find out what they really want to read about and what articles would appeal to them.

Focusing on Retirement

Retirement is a funny thing. It can come along early when you are in your 50s or much later, especially as governments keep upping the statutory retirement age. In years past, people expected to spend their lives in a particular career and retire out of it at around 65 years of age. It was always looked on as a downward slide, a kind of marker that denoted the end of work life and being two steps away from death's door. But that's not the case anymore, people are living longer, careers can be shorter and retirement is more of a time in life to have freedom and follow pursuits that you have always been interested in but never had the time to take up.

Over 50s magazines reflect this in their upbeat and positive attitude. After retirement, you can do anything and their pages are packed with articles that prove it. I once wrote an article about buying gifts for ladies who were due to retire but there wasn't a mention of a carriage clock anywhere!

'Retirement can sometimes be seen as a time to go slow but for many people, it is a chance to do something that they have always wanted to but never had the time before. So what does your gift receiver want to do? Have they got a bucket list? They might have always wanted to fly a plane or go up in a hot air balloon. You can buy vouchers to give them a day out they will never forget. Have they got grandchildren that they would love to treat? What about a day out at a theme park or nature reserve?' (Overblog, 2011).

Living Abroad

Some magazines for the senior readership contain articles about living abroad and some magazines about living abroad contain articles for a senior readership! Not every older person has had the income to purchase a second home but some have or they may have moved to live with family or they may head to the sun for six months of the year.

There are opportunities to write about life in other countries including topics like learning the language, what to do about health care, where to meet other expats and humorous tales of living away from home. Other people are interested in whether the move has worked out or what pitfalls to avoid, especially when they are considering living abroad themselves. If you have any experience of living in another country then you might like to try writing this type of lifestyle article.

Travel

Travel articles focus on trips where being aged isn't an issue. Places to visit, things to see and do, places to stay - all have to be checked out so that if visitors do have special needs or require help with access then these don't present a problem. I remember taking my Nan to a stately home without checking out the amount of stairs she would have to climb. They were nearly beyond me, let alone her! Luckily they had a hidden lift that had been installed in the 50s. It was a great piece of architecture and it got us up and down so she could look at every room. Any article that you write should cover aspects like this that will make a visit easier.

Although travel articles should take into consideration the restrictions that aging may bring, they don't have to be boring. Older people still want exciting adventures and memorable outings so consider writing about travel pieces that include themed holidays, train journeys, cruising adventures and all-in-one packages.

Food and Wine

Food can cover a wide range of writing from recipes and healthy diets to eating out and dining in. Remember as people get older they may have been advised to watch their diets and recipe writing for this age range can reflect that. Typical diets include foods that are low in sodium, cholesterol-busting or cancer-fighting. Readers also like to know which restaurants can cater for their needs as well as places that the whole family can visit that will provide a range of meals.

Wine articles are also popular with this age group. Perhaps that's because they have required better taste than the local supermarket's cheapo plonk! If this is your passion - to write about it not drink it - you'll need to hone your senses and be able to write like a professional wine taster. If you've never done this before, there are often wine appreciation evening classes or clubs where you can pick up the necessary skills. You need to be able to write about aroma, colour, texture and taste - not only the first sip but the lingering tones that caress your palate. It's really quite descriptive writing and one that you must have some knowledge about, like which wine goes with what food and which vintage is recommended and what years were best.

Dating

Dating is still as much of an interest to older people as it is to the younger members of our society, but it can be especially difficult for people who no longer want to frequent bars and clubs and the usual dating venues. I wrote this for the wellbeing section of Vista's website which is an online magazine for women.

'As we get older we tend to stick to the same routines; work, housework, eat, sleep. If we don't do something different, we won't meet new people and be open to a new relationship. Think about trying an evening class. Is there a local community centre near you that offers courses or workshops that you could attend? What about a fitness class, cookery group or hobby club you could join? That way if you meet someone new, you already have a shared interest and will have something in common. Ever thought of volunteering? The man of your dreams could be helping out at your local church or

charity. Lots of charities need help with fund-raising and other day-to-day activities. If you have a few hours to spare, volunteering will get you out of the house and meeting new people.' (Vista, 2012)

Dating becomes even more complicated when you have kids, grandkids, or have been married once or twice before and so any articles for this market should counter the issues that older people come across when trying to find a partner later in life.

Try this Exercise: The Dating Game

Imagine you are a single man in your sixties and you would love to meet someone to share the rest of your years with. You've been married once before and have two sons that live in different parts of the world. You don't have any close family living near you but you do enjoy walking your dog and stopping in a cafe for an herbal tea on your way home where you read the latest crime novel and watch the world go by.

Think about it for awhile. Where could you meet new people? How do you get back into the dating game? How difficult or easy would it be? Write an article based on your thoughts and feelings that will give advice to other elderly men in a similar situation.

Health

We've mentioned health before and yes, it is inevitable that magazines for the older age group are going to cover health. Topics dealt with are more typical to older people like dealing with arthritis, failing eyesight and hearing, digestive problems and the menopause. There are also articles on less severe issues that affect the older age group like loss of appetite, lack of sleep and how to stay healthy and warm during the winter months.

Coping with long-term illness is something that you could write about if you have experienced it and have the knowledge to write about the illness and what different remedies and coping strategies you have used. Health articles are still upbeat for the over 50s but there is also an acknowledgement that some things aren't just going to go away and that it's about coping with them rather than curing them. There is also a focus on having regular check-ups as you get older and demystifying the techniques and words that doctors use.

Remember that health covers lots of topics and the over 50s still want to read about exercise tips, products that can make life easier, living a healthy lifestyle and looking after themselves.

Telling Life Stories

A lot of over 50s magazines contain real life readers' stories and they ask readers to send in their tales to various sections. Memories and recollections make up a large amount of articles for this market and editors are always open to ideas for new articles. Flick through the pages of some of these magazines and you will see ads inviting readers to send in their stories. Do your market research to see what type of life stories they are looking for. Do they want relationship tales, holiday experiences or features about coping with an illness? I'm sure that you have a story that you could share with readers. This can be one of the easiest ways to see your work in print so pick one of the sections and give it a go.

Nostalgia Writing

Although life stories are nostalgic, there are other articles that look at the way things were from a wider point of view. Tales of growing-up in a particular place, childhood games, the food we used to eat, the school meals we were served and the cars we used to drive have all featured in nostalgic writing. Again, some magazines have specific sections for this style of writing but you can always suggest your own.

Nostalgic writing is about marking the differences between now and then. Think back to your childhood and teenage years and make some comparisons between those years and today.

What were better about them? What was worse? Has life improved or was living better then? See what ideas you can come up with and try fleshing the best one out as a full article.

Writing about Family History

Family history enthusiasts have their own magazines and you could decide to try one of these if you have a feature length article in mind but over 50s magazines do sometimes take family history pieces if they are unusual or different in some way. War stories are particularly popular and many of the older generation still remember the Second World War and took part in it. If your family has a story of courage and resilience, could you write about it? You may need photos or images of documents to go with it so be prepared to do a little more homework.

Do you come from a circus background, a racing family or did your family set up and run the same business for generations? What stories do your family have that you could draw on, investigate and research more and then use for a really interesting article?

Writing for the over 50s has lots to offer lifestyle writers so if you are interested in this market, seek out copies of magazines and have a look at websites that are geared to the older generations. Don't forget to talk to older people to find out what their interests are, what is important in their lives and what you could write about for them.

Chapter Eleven

Writing Lifestyle Articles for the Web

Throughout this book, I have mentioned websites and writing lifestyle articles not only for print but for web viewing as well. Whatever type of lifestyle article you hope to write, there are opportunities to post your work onto the World Wide Web. It can be a great way to build your portfolio, gain you readers and even provide you with an income.

The Difference between Print and Web articles

For a start, web articles are far shorter than print articles. Ok so some print columns might be short but an average length article will be in the region of 1,000 words whereas a web article can be as little as 250. The average length is usually around 400-500 words. The nature of browsing means that people just don't stay on a page for hours and hours. They click on an article title and scan it to see if it will contain the information there are looking for. If they don't find key words in the first few seconds of reading, that's it, they'll go onto something else. So writing web articles is all about packing in lots of easy-to-understand information in bite size pieces.

There is a kind of impatience with the Internet. People expect it to turn up what information they need instantly and they won't spend hours reading web articles. When we read a web page, it's at a distance that our eyes are not used to; a TV is further away, a book is closer. We tend to look down the left side of a page to find keywords and then scan horizontally to see if there's any further interesting information. If we have to page down and down to continue reading, we get fed up and go on to find something shorter. Saying that, there are longer articles on the Internet but people tend to download them to read later on or to print them out.

Do you need to be Computer Savvy?

You need to have a certain amount of computer skills but by no means do you need to be an expert. For instance, one of the online magazines I write for has a writer's dashboard where you enter your article. It's well laid out with boxes for the title, subheading, main body of text and image to accompany your text. There's a help function and a programme manager who you can contact if you have any issues. Guidelines are provided from what to write about to how to insert hyperlinks and images. You need to be comfortable enough with computers to use such a system but once you've tried it a couple of times, you will be using it with ease.

One thing I will say is if you are writing for the Internet, you need to have a good connection. I don't and it can be extremely annoying when you have a picture to post but your provider has slowed you down. Not all web editors will ask for images to accompany your articles but some will. That means you need to be able to download pictures from sites such as Morguefile or Flickr and then upload them with your article. If your connection is slow, it won't be able to manage photo file sizes.

Writing Lifestyle Articles for the Web

In my book, *The Writer's Internet*, I go into some detail about writing for the web. Here are some key points taken from that book.

The most important information goes at the top of a web article

The first sentence should answer any question that has been asked

Short, compact paragraphs are essential

Sentences should be simple and concise

Subheadings are used to regularly break up paragraphs - more than they would appear in a printed article

Use Arial or Times New Roman fonts unless otherwise indicated

Don't use italics, change fonts, colour words or make any other changes to your text that makes it look fussy and unreadable

Use Plain English, no jargon

Use short words instead of long-winded ones

Cut out all extraneous words

Don't underline - that's for links

Links to websites can be included (and underlined!)

Don't use block capitals - it's like shouting

Key words can be used so a search engine can index the article

Be absolutely clear and concise, utilising every word to maximum effect

No text speak or emoticons please!

Writing for the Internet is all about keeping it short and sweet and to the point. Crisp, clear and concise is the rule. When you have such a low word count, you really don't have room to use flowery description or extraneous words. That doesn't mean to say it should be simple and basic but then again, you don't know the literacy level of your readership so don't get carried away with big, long words! Even if you are writing a technical or academic piece, it has to be understandable by a wide range of readers so limit your jargon and use Plain English.

What can you Write about?

Near enough, anything! When you look at job sites, they will give you some idea of what content providers and other websites are looking for. You may be asked to pick categories so you can hone in on a subject that really interests you and that you will have lots of ideas for. For instance, I worked for Wikio Experts and wrote in their arts and crafts, education, home and wellbeing sections. The articles I've written recently for Vista are primarily in the wellbeing section but also relationships and the home. So that you can see exactly how a web article looks when you submit it, here's one I prepared earlier!

Changing Your Career

A new year can mean a new you and what better way is there to start a new year than by changing your career. This is the time to start thinking about what you really want to do with your life and start taking steps towards a job change in the future. It may not happen overnight but you can start planning for a career change.

Dust off your Resume

When thinking about changing your career, have a look at some employment websites like Monster or Indeed. What type of jobs are on offer? Are there openings in the career you would like to follow? Check out what is available and what skills or qualifications you need. Dust off your resume and give it a fresh look. Update your information and bring all your experience and skills up-to-date. Make sure that your qualifications and skills, the ones most relevant for your new career, stand out and make you look like the ideal candidate.

Take a Course

If you are thinking about changing your career but feel that you may need new qualifications or certification, look around to see what courses are available in the New Year. There could be some short courses that you could take to update your resume or distance learning courses that will prepare you for a new career path. Check out local education centers to see what's on offer or ask for local college adult education prospectuses to see if there are any evening classes coming up. You can start to re-skill and qualify in new areas as you start your job search.

Practice Interview Skills

Start practicing your interview skills. You may be a little rusty with these or you may not have had much success previously. Find a friend you can practice with and become more comfortable about answering questions. When you are changing your career, interviewers will expect you to know something about the industry or company you hope to work for. While you are job-seeking, spend the time reading about the latest developments and trends so that you come across as knowledgeable in your field at interview. Treat yourself to a new set of interview clothes in the sales so that you feel confident and smart when you talk to prospective employers.

Changing your career takes planning and organisation. Dust off your resume, browse job sites, consider taking new qualifications and practice your interview skills. By putting time into planning your new career path, you will be well on the way to changing your career.

This article was used by Vista, had an accompanying image of a young woman and came in at around 400 words. It has a five paragraph structure which is typical to web writing. The first paragraph introduces the subject, the next three discuss the topic and the fifth summarises the whole article. Easy, eh?

All the lifestyle topics are covered - travel, parenting, food, cars, computers - so it's a matter of you deciding what you want to concentrate on and looking for work in that area. If you are hoping to write for the harder markets to break into, like food and fashion writing, then having web articles with your name on them will showcase your skills and add to your portfolio when you are contacting print editors.

Try this Exercise: The Web Article

So using the structure as it appears above, have a go at writing your own web article. Remember the bulleted points above and write crisp, clear and concise copy. Split it into five paragraphs each with their own sub-heading and add a title. Write not more than 500 words on a topic of your choice. If you have been inspired by one of the previous chapters, pick that topic and give it a go.

Where to find Work

There are lots of different sites offering work to writers who can write short, informative and practical lifestyle articles. There are job sites where freelance work opportunities are posted, bid sites where you bid for a job amongst other writers and content providers that you can sign up with and see what assignments are available.

All of them have different rates of pay and ways of working. Some ask you just to provide short articles, others ask you to post to a blog or manage your own topics web page.

Some of the best freelance sites are:

About: www.about.com
Craigs List: www.craigslist.com
Constant Content: www.constant-content.com
Demand Media studios: www.demandstudios.com
Families: www.families.com
Freelance Writing: www.freelancewriting.com
Freelance Writing Gigs: www.freelancewritinggigs.com
Hubpages: www.hubpages.com
Online Writing Jobs: www.online-writing-jobs.com
Skyword: www.skyword.com
Squidoo: www.squidoo.com
Textbroker: www.textbroker.com, www.textbroker.co.uk
Wisegeek: www.wisegeek.com
Words of Worth: www.wordsofworth.co.uk
Writing World: www.writing-world.com

Before you apply for any work on these sites, look at the articles of other writers on their web pages to gauge their tone, length and style. You will be asked for a sample of your writing for many of these jobs so choose a topic that you know they cover but don't currently have an article on and follow any guidelines they give you.

Using SEO

SEO stands for search engine optimisation, a process that makes websites visible to search engines. Search engines crawl the Internet looking for keywords so that they can index them and produce their search results. Some online writing jobs will ask you to add keywords into your articles. Say you write an article about changing your career, 'career' could be the keyword that has to be repeated a certain amount of times within the text. Or you write about dealing with depression and 'depression' will have to feature several times in the body of the article. You will usually be told how many times and what exactly the keywords are but other content providers might ask you for SEO friendly copy straight up.

The trick with writing SEO text is to think about what words a person would use to look up an article. Say you wanted to find an article on the best beauty products for mature skin. Your keywords are 'beauty', 'mature skin' and 'products'. You could also add in related terms like 'skin care' or 'aging'. To come up with keywords, think about what a person would ask a search engine to look for in order to come up with a list of search results. Job opportunities often come up for lifestyle writers that can provide articles that are SEO friendly. If you are seriously considering web writing then learn a little more about SEO to increase your chances of work.

Revenue v. pay per post

There are two ways in which most writers get paid for their

online work. The first is pay per post. Simply, you write an article and get paid for it. Beware that rates for web articles can be extremely low so always check out the payment rates before you do the work. I once wrote for a company that only paid £2.50 per article of 250 words so that's only a penny a word. The thing was the articles were easy to write and I could write several in an hour. Still it's not much. The most I have been paid is $30 per piece which is much nicer on the bank balance and mounts up to a tidy sum at the end of a month. If the payment is low, you will need to weigh up whether it would still be good as it will give you writing credits to your name or whether you'd rather take your services elsewhere.

Revenue is another method also referred to as pay per click. You don't receive any money upfront but your article earns every time someone clicks onto it. Writers have mixed feelings about this way of earning. Some prefer the upfront payment, however small it is, whilst others have managed to create an income through revenue. The upside of revenue is that your article earns for as long as it stays on a website so it can continue to earn for an indefinite amount of time whereas pay per post is one payment and that's your lot. Before taking any online work, do check in what way your earnings are calculated. Web writing won't make you a millionaire but it can provide a nice stream of income.

Getting Paid

Content providers, website owners and online editors usually pay online too. By this I mean that they will use a service like PayPal to lodge your earnings into. Setting up an account with PayPal (www.paypal.com) is straightforward and will only take a few minutes. Your account name is your email address so when you are asked for your PayPal details, you just give that. No one else can enter your account and although people might be wary of having an online banking account, it is a really safe and secure system that enables you to get paid for your online work. You can then spend it straight from your account by paying for goods online with PayPal or you can transfer it into your regular bank account.

Some work for the Web will require you to send invoices, others won't. Many content providers have a financial section attached to your writer's dashboard or page so you can regularly check your earnings. If you are required to send invoices, remember to number and date them. You can set up a template on your computer so you only have to change a few details every time and have them ready to email off to your employer. Remember to change the file name every time you send out a new invoice. I'm terrible for over-writing things which means I can never find my own copy when I go looking for it.

Blogging

I've mentioned blogging several times in relation to building your portfolio but what is a blog? It's really just a regularly updated website presented like a diary or a journal. You can write daily entries, monthly entries or update it whenever you like but you will build more of a readership if you write regularly so that people think great, I'll check that every Friday or the first Monday of every month - whenever you choose to update it.

You don't have to write reams and reams of text. Blogs are usually kept short - about the same length as a web article so they come across as bite-sized pieces of information rather than pages a reader has to trawl through. They can also include photos, video clips and other images to entertain your readers.

There are some websites that provide templates of blogs and host them for you so that you can start writing your own blog straightaway. Have a look at:

Tumblr (www.tumblr.com)
Posterous (www.posterous.com)

Google's Blogger (www.blogger.com)
Wordpress (www.wordpress.org)

You should also check out the blogs of other writers to see what they write about and how they present their material. Check out:

Victoria Everman (www.victoria-e.com)
Jessica Benavides Canepa (www.jbcanepa.com/blog)
Signe Langford (www.signelangford.weebly.com/blog)
Dana Damato (www.danadamato.com/blog)
Tim Ferriss (www.fourhourworkingweek.com/blog)
Heather Clawson (www.habituallychic.blogspot.com)
Sara Ross (www.msadventuresinitaly.com/blog)

Don't forget to add your blog information to any CV, biography or contact information you send out to editors and publishers. If you have Facebook, Twitter or LinkedIn accounts add those too so that you can be easily contacted and samples of your work can be browsed. The more you promote yourself as a writer online, the more work will come your way and we all want that, don't we?

Chapter Twelve

Researching your Writing

When you write lifestyle articles, you will have some knowledge of the subject you are writing about but there is always room to learn more. From time to time, you will need to check facts, get quotes and talk to experts or professionals to find out more information. Researching is as much a part of article writing as the writing itself. Some writers love it, others hate it but we all have to do it!

Where to find Research Materials

Nowadays the Internet is the best place to go. You can be typing away and need to check out some facts and with a few clicks of a button, there's your answer. It's one big giant reference guide at your fingertips. You'll find anything and everything there from news stories to archives, free e-books to online documents. You can also check article directories to see what else has been written on your chosen subject and to give you ideas for where the gaps are that will provide you with a writing opportunity.

But the Internet isn't the only place to go. Building up your own reference library is a great way to have books and information on hand. Start collecting reference books on the topics you are interested in writing about. You don't have to spend a fortune. Go to second-hand book stores, car boot sales and charity shops to build up your collection. Ask friends to keep you in mind when they are clearing out their bookshelves and look out for any discounted book sales or library clear-outs. This way you will gradually build up a ready reference to mull over when you're working on ideas or when you have an article in progress.

Attending events, workshops, shows and seminars is a great way to research and make contact with other people that might provide pertinent quotes and expert information. Say you're interested in travel writing then go to holiday events, living abroad exhibitions and travel shows. If you want to write about gardening and outdoor living, make sure you attend any gardening shows or green fairs that are on. Interested in cars? Then make sure you go to launches of new models, national events and motoring extravaganzas. Often there will be workshops or talks at these events where you can pick up more information and listen to an expert speak. You can always introduce yourself afterwards and tell them you're a lifestyle writer that would like to stay in contact with them in the future. Pick up contact details from the people you meet and the companies that are showing their products. You never know when you will need them.

Some areas of writing will benefit by you actually going out to visit places. Travel writing, of course, is where this mainly comes in. You can't write about a spa break or an adventure holiday without trying it out. Neither can you review a restaurant nor a hotel without going there, so some research will mean savouring the delights and the not-so-delightful places you are going to write about.

Finding Facts

Although the Internet is your one click stop, everything you find on it will need checking. Why? Because no-one edits the Internet. You can write any old thing on a website and the fact police won't knock on your door if you've got it wrong. So don't just check one site, check a few, especially for things like dates, people and places. Make absolutely sure that you get them right or you will have an editor breathing down your neck and readers that are unhappy with your work.

That's where having a physical book collection will help for reference. I have certain books that I use all the time to check people and places; one is a world history book that always gives me historical background information and makes sure I get my dates right. I also gather factual books on all sorts of topics for only a few Euros each at a local car boot sale so I can refer to them as I'm writing.

You might remember in the travel writing chapter, I suggested collecting leaflets, tickets and other seemingly random bits of paper on your travels. This is also true of places and products you visit or test. Gather company brochures, technical specifications, hotel guides and leaflets whenever you are out and about researching your articles. These will give you facts to add into your writing.

Don't forget to look up statistics and reports online. Government surveys, marketing reports and independent researchers all publish their findings and these can be used to add authority and authenticity to your writing. A lot of information is downloadable but you can also contact central statistics offices or government bodies to find out what publications may be of relevance to your research.

Finding Stories

Every type of lifestyle story includes human interest stories and tales of readers' experiences. Your first point of call for stories is with your family and friends. Be an eager listener and pay attention when you hear them relating a story that you just might be able to use. Of course you will need to ask permission from anybody whose story you want to write up but friends and family may also have ideas that will lead you on to researching new article ideas.

Listen in to other people's conversations. Whether you are on the train, waiting in a queue or picking the kids up for school, listen out for what people are talking about. What is being debated? What issues are people concerned with? Are there problems or concerns they have that would make a great how-to article or a top ten tips piece?

Keep an eye on the news. Read a newspaper on a regularly basis even if it's just a Sunday one for possible article ideas. Subscribe to news feeds on the Internet, especially those covering soft news and human interest stories and sign up to email newsletters from sites that cover your topics. And don't forget to read the magazines you hope to write for. They might cover a story that gives you an idea for a different way to cover the topic or a new angle that doesn't seem to have been addressed.

Keeping up-to-date with your Interests

I mentioned signing up to email newsletters before as a way of keeping up with new trends and latest developments. Keeping up-to-date with your interests is important so that you know what people will be interested in reading and what new topics you can cover. Read magazines that could offer writing opportunities but also to keep ahead of what else has been written and to help you see where the gaps are for you to fill. Bookmark websites that bring you the latest news and regularly check in with them to see what's being written. Be always on the look-out for stories and article ideas so that you are never stuck for something to write or research further.

Where to go on the Internet

The world is your oyster or alternatively a huge great cosmos of things to look up and read about. It can be a big wide world to browse and sometimes it's hard to know where to start. Here are some reference sites you can use to begin your search:

All Experts: www.allexperts.com
Answers: www.answers.com
Encyclopedia: www.encyclopedia.com
How Stuff Works: www.howstuffworks.com
Refdesk: www.refdesk.com

Reference: www.reference.com

Wikipedia: www.wikipedia.com

You can also narrow down your searches by using an online web directory. This will give you a more comprehensive list of results than an average web browser would. Check out:

Best of the Web Directory: www.botw.org

Exact Seek: www.exactseek.com

The Open Directory Project: www.dmoz.org

Webotopia: www.webotopia.org

There is also such a thing as an article directory where hundreds and hundreds of articles are listed for your perusal. Have a browse at:

Amazines: www.amazines.com

Article Alley: www.articlealley.com

Buzzle: www.buzzle.com

Ezine Articles: www.ezinearticles.com

Go Articles: www.goarticles.com

Helium: www.helium.com

The more you use the Internet for research, the more you will know what sites to head to for information. I use Wikipedia a lot for basic information (although not all pages are verified) as each entry also has other websites listed that you can go to, so I usually start my search there but end up somewhere completely different.

Interviewing in Depth

To add more information to your writing, especially quotes, you can interview interesting and knowledgeable people to give your writing more depth. For instance, I once wrote a parenting article about whether teachers should show affection to their pupils and if so, how much. It came after a news article suggested that teachers of primary school children should not hug or touch a child if they are distressed. The whole teacher/child relationship topic is one that is hotly debated so I wanted to interview a teacher to see how they felt. I contacted a teacher's organisation who put me in touch with a lady who had agreed to be interviewed on the subject and I also interviewed a parent for their viewpoint and used both of their points of view in my writing.

When you are thinking of who to interview, ask yourself who will know most about the topic? Is there an organisation or association that can put you in contact with an expert? Are there two sides to the story? You might need to include opposing views. Say you are writing about organic food, you could include a quote from a grower who believes that organic food is the healthier option and another quote from an advocate of genetically modified foods who thinks GM foods are better than organic. Contrasting viewpoints make for compelling reading but this means you need to find experts with different opinions to interview.

How to Prepare

Before you set out to interview someone for your lifestyle article, you can prepare by doing a bit of homework! First find out as much about the person as you can from the Internet. They might have a Facebook page or a LinkedIn profile that you can look at, or their business or organisation might have a website that will give you some background information on them.

Know your subject so that you don't come across as being disinterested or unknowledgeable. You will probably only be writing about a topic because of your interest in it but I know I've had to cover things I haven't had a clue about so read up on your subject matter first.

Have an aim in mind. Don't just meet up with someone and

chat away for two hours taking notes and then get home and realise you haven't got anything worth using. Decide before you go to an interview what information you need. Planning your questions will help you to focus in on the details that will make your lifestyle article interesting and readable.

What to Ask

That depends on what you are writing about! But what I will say is use open questions. It's no good asking questions that your interviewee can just say yes or no to - they won't get you anywhere. You need to ask questions that require a more detailed response. Try questions that start with

How did you feel when...?
What made you...?
Why is....?
Can you describe...?

Try this Exercise: Grab an Interviewee

Some writers don't like interviewing much. They feel very self-conscious about contacting people and saying they are a writer and would like to interview them but the more you do it, the easier it becomes. Practice on a friend or member of your family first. If you want to write about parenting, pick someone who's a mum. Want to write about teen fashion? Then grab a teenager to interview. Write out ten open questions on a topic that you would like to write about. Then get started! Try taking notes as they speak and you will see how tricky it is to get everything down word for word. It's a good idea to invest in a digital recorder if you think you are going to be interviewing a lot and this will give you the chance to try it out.

Conducting an Interview in Person

So how do you go about interviewing in person? Arrange a time and place that is comfortable and suitable for your interviewee. Arrive before they do and organise yourself so that you are ready for when they get there. Introduce yourself and explain the reason why you want to interview them. You may have already touched on this during a phone call or email but put your interviewee at ease by talking about your writing and how much they can help you.

Begin by checking their personal details, especially the spelling of their name or their title. Ask them a bit about themselves so they begin to relax before you begin asking trickier questions. Use positive and encouraging body language like smiling and nodding to put your interviewee at ease. Even if you are taking notes or fiddling with a digital recorder, maintain eye contact so that they know you are paying attention and are interested in what they are saying. Ask your open questions and if you need clarification of a certain point or want more details about something they've just said, don't be afraid to ask. When you have all your answers, finish the interview by thanking your interviewee and making sure they have your contact details.

Asking Permission

Always ask if it's ok to use a person's words in writing before you add them into your article. Often interviews go off on a tangent and things are said that are off-the-record. Your interviewee might regret something they have said or only want you to use some stuff and not others. I always send a quick email after an interview that highlights what quotes I'm going to use and double-check that my interviewee is ok with that. If I have a preview or proof of the article, I also send them a copy so they can see in which context their words are going to be used but this isn't always possible.

Interviewing by Email

The above includes information about interviewing someone in person but you may prefer to interview by email or your inter-viewee might prefer this type of contact. Many of us are so busy with our lives that it's hard to find time to fit things in. However, email interviews can be completed by people who otherwise wouldn't be able to take time out of their busy schedules or live too far away to make a personal interview possible.

Keep email interviews brief. Ever had an email from someone that went on for pages? It's like reading articles on the Internet; we don't expect to be reading them an hour later. This will test your ability to come up with questions that will give usable responses. I usually suggest just sending five questions initially. You can always follow up with more questions or ask your inter-viewee to give you some more details about something you have asked. The joy of getting your responses by email is that you have your quotes in type. You can copy and paste directly into your article and will never have a problem over misquoting.

On the other hand, if you are interviewing in person, please don't rely just on a notebook. I used to use an old Dictaphone - one you put tapes in - but these are near enough obsolete now. Invest in a digital recorder so that you capture what your inter-viewee is saying word for word rather than trying to fill in the blanks later.

Writing it Up

Once you've gathered all your research materials, interviewed for quotes and planned what you are going to write, you need to sit down and write it - obviously! So it's time to snap out of research mode and into writing mode and sometimes this can be difficult. I know I find it hard to switch off from research and actually start the process of writing. I think oh, I'll just look up one more thing, then two hours later I'm still browsing the Internet. So I time my research to finish at the end of a day and then the following morning, it's time to write - no ifs or buts or maybes and if I'm tempted to just check one more thing... I tell myself I can only do that after I've written the first draft so at least there's something down on paper.

Organising your Research

I use a cool software package called One Note by Microsoft. You can type in notes, cut and paste relevant passages from the Internet and use it like a computerised filing cabinet. It's great for organising longer articles or book proposals where the research mounts up but you are not sure what you will actually use.

I've also got box files, folders, filing cabinets and those notebooks with dividers in for separate sections. I use folders for newspaper and magazine clippings, box files for other things like tickets, leaflets and brochures. And then there are all the computer files. Every few weeks I tidy up Word documents and downloaded material into folders and back these up onto a memory stick. If you have most of your research on your computer, save it somewhere else too just in case it goes kaput. Invest in an external hard drive or burn completed articles to disc - whatever way you want to save a copy, do just that. I have gone through laptops and computers like nobody's business and I have lost volumes of work in the process. Especially if you are working on a book, you need to regularly save your chapters elsewhere so if lightning strikes, you've still got a copy!

Chapter Thirteen

Getting Published

So what's the point in having loads of ideas if you don't get your work published? Your ultimate goal is of course to see your work in print whether it's in the pages of a magazine or on the pages of a website. Whether to include your work will be an editor's decision but you can help your article by presenting it in the best possible way.

Presenting your Manuscript

Your article is written and it's ready to be submitted to a magazine in hard copy. You want it to look as good as possible on an editor's desk and stand out from all the other manuscripts they'll have to read but don't go using fluorescent green paper, perfume sprayed sheets or coloured, bold text!

There is a format for presentation that manuscripts generally follow. Editors will expect your work to be submitted in this appropriate manner. You will need to make up a title page that includes information that an editor can glance over. This goes on top of your article. A title page has your name, address and contact information on the left hand side, the word count on the right and the title of the article and your name centred in the middle. This shows the importance of titles. Apart from reading a cover or query letter, it's the first thing an editor sees and it helps them to decide whether it sounds interesting enough for them to read more or whether it's more of the same old that they have already published.

On the next sheet, which will be the first of your article, put your address on the top left-hand side and centre the article's title and your name before starting on the main body of writing. On the following and subsequent pages you need to write your surname, reference to your article and page number in the topmost right-hand corner. Use the header command if using Word to create a heading like *Watkins - Learn the Language (2)*. You needn't add the full title unless it is short enough to but instead use key words from it.

On the last page of your manuscript, add in the copyright symbol ©, your name and the year. This can be added as a footer, like © *Sarah-Beth Watkins, 2012*. There is some debate over whether copyright is needed on articles these days. If you're working for a website or have signed up to provide content for a website provider, then copyright will already be covered in your contract or writing guidelines. For print articles, it's up to you but it doesn't hurt to finish your article with copyright information.

Throughout your article you should use double spacing, a regular font like Times New Roman and make clear where new paragraphs start. Either indent each new paragraph or leave a space between paragraphs. Always use clean, white A4 size paper and bind your work using a paperclip and not staples.

Once your article is well presented, you need just add a cover letter before posting it out. A short letter addressed to the editor or other contact name you might have gleaned from your market research must accompany your article. If you want your manuscript back, enclose an SAE or international reply coupon for ease of reply.

The Cover Letter

Once upon a time there was a clear distinction between a cover letter and a query letter but electronic submissions have blurred the two. If you are sending your article on paper to a magazine, you will need a typed cover letter that introduces yourself and your work. It should contain your contact details, a short synopsis of your article and a few lines about your writing experience or your credentials and why you are the best person to write such an article. Say you write an interior design piece and you have run your own company for several years or you graduated from design college; mention this when you are approaching an editor. If you've written about travel for a website or posted reviews, add this information to your cover letter for a travel article. Mention to an editor anything that makes you seem like the best person to write that article. Sell yourself and you will go some way towards selling your work too.

The Query Letter

I can't think of any query that I have sent into a magazine recently that hasn't been by email. In bygone days, the query letter was the first thing you sent into an editor and if you received a reply, you submitted your full manuscript. It still has the same function but isn't really a formal letter anymore but a few lines of an email.

It still has to give details of the article you hope to sell to the editor and some background information about yourself though. You don't have to write your life history but a few lines that give an editor some indication of your experience and why you are the person to write this article. A query I wrote recently went something like this:

After reading about your publication in Writing Magazine, I wanted to contact you regarding an idea I have for a full length article that you might be interested in. The article 'Simple Homemade Wines' is a practical, easy-to-follow guide on how to make your own wine at home using the simplest ingredients. I learned the art of wine-making from my grandparents and this article includes some of their most successful recipes.

I am a freelance writer with over 20 years of experience writing lifestyle articles for magazines such as Take a Break, Your New Baby, Wikio Experts and Overblog. Please let me know if you would like to read the full article.

They did and it was published several months later. Queries don't need to take up much of your time but do keep a track of them. Try not to send out the same query to different magazines at one time. I know it's tempting when you can just send out a heap of emails at one go but if you get ten replies that say, yes, send it to us and three of those actually want to publish it then you've got a problem. The joy of emailing queries is that you usually hear back within days so if they don't want to read your article you can send a query to another editor.

Be prepared to come up with some other ideas instantly. I recently sent an email to one editor who said they had used a similar idea recently but what else did I have to offer? I had to reply to that email within a few days listing three or four other articles I thought I could write. Always have a few ideas at the ready in case you are asked for the same.

Email Submissions

A lot of magazines accept submissions by email these days, usually after you have already checked in with the editor to see if your idea is suitable and if they want to see more.

Whether you are sending your article to a magazine or website, the same rules go for presentation unless their guidelines say otherwise. They will often have these ready to download from their website and will contain information on how to submit your work electronically.

Most of the editors I have sent work to have asked for a Word attachment but I have come across some editors who don't like opening attachments, presumably in case they contain viruses. In that case, I have had to copy my article into the body of an email and send it that way. It can make for a very long and unwieldy email but if that's what the editor wants...

Where to Find Magazine and Publishers Details

UK magazine editors and book publishers are listed in *The*

Writers' and Artists' Yearbook and *The Writer's Handbook*. For US information, check out *Writer's Market* published by Writer's Digest Books. All of these books come out yearly so make sure to look up the latest details in the newest edition. For information on websites that provide work for writers, check out my previous book *The Writer's Internet.*

You will also find information online by googling magazine and publishers' websites and regularly reading sites for writers that list market opportunities. Also pick up writing magazines that are available in your country. The UK has *Writing Magazine* that contains a market news section with several leads for articles and books wanted in each edition. And of course, read the magazines and websites you hope to write for, being on the lookout for any mention of stories or articles wanted.

Serial Rights

You might come across serial rights in any contract you sign with a magazine or website. I used to add what serial rights were on offer to the title page of all of my articles but I tend to leave that up to editors to decide what they are buying now. Serial rights are a way of saying what rights you are selling and in which country so if you are selling your article to a British magazine, you can put 'First British Serial Rights Offered' on your title page under the word count or the abbreviation 'FBSR offered'. Or the name of the country in which the targeted magazine is published.

This means you can sell your article to magazines across the world at any one time by indicating what rights you are selling. You could send it to Britain, America, France, Spain, and so on if you have found possible markets by offering rights based in that country. You offer first rights when your article has never been published elsewhere. You can then offer second rights when your article has already been sold once. Subsequently you use second rights whether it's the second or fiftieth time you are selling your article. So you offer first rights when you send out your article for the first time. If that sells and a year or so down the line, you wanted to try to sell your article again to a new market then you offer that market second rights.

If you are selling to a national newspaper you will be offering 'world rights'. This is because newspapers are shipped out to different parts of the world. A newspaper may also want to reproduce your article in another one of their international publications. Writing for the Internet also carries its own rights and they are 'all electronic rights'. You will be selling all electronic rights to give them complete use of your article in any electronic form. As well as appearing on a website your article might become accessible to download to a tablet, used as mobile info or stored by the publisher by electronic means. As the web is worldwide, you sell all rights. Only one website is going to carry your work at any one time.

As I've said, I usually just sign over rights when I sign a contract. I recently sold an article to a North American magazine so there was a clause that indicated that they were purchasing North American rights. If you think you will be sending your article around the world by all means include what rights you are offering on your title page (under the word count) or like me, you can leave it to those who are more fluent in legalese.

Chapter Fourteen

The Lifestyle Book

Every now and again an idea comes up for an article that's so much bigger than a few hundred words. All of a sudden you realise that you have the makings of a book. Writing a lifestyle book takes commitment and perseverance and a whole lot of time. You're going to have to write more than 30,000 words which will take a few months at least. But just think! Your own book with your own name on the cover. For a writer, there's no greater joy than having your work published in book form.

Finding an Idea

Have you got an idea already? Is there a topic that you are really passionate about that fires your imagination and makes you feel like you could write for hours? If you have already settled on a lifestyle topic that you want to write about or have even started writing about it, then you might find your mind wandering onto bigger book size things!

Start an ideas book, not just for your articles, but for your book ideas. I use one of those tiny little notepads just for book ideas no matter how random they are. I've got non-fiction ideas, full length novels, short stories and poetry book ideas. Whenever I'm stuck thinking about my next project, I flick through it to see what I could work on next.

Don't worry if your idea hasn't come to you yet. Once you are writing lifestyle articles and looking for ideas, book size ones will come along too. One tip is to think of the title first. It can always be changed later on but its good practice to condense an idea into a title which could lead to a book proposal to work on. When I walk the dog, I try to think of titles as I'm getting some exercise. Whenever you have thinking time, try out a few titles too and see whether you think you could write a whole book based on what you've come up with.

Have you got enough Information?

An idea is easy to flesh out into an article of 500 words, more difficult if it is 1,000 but a book length idea? Well, that needs work. This is where you will start to realise whether you really have a book idea or whether it would be better as a series of shorter articles. A book is going to be roughly ten chapters long, 3,000 words per chapter - that's a skinny 30,000 word book but a book nonetheless. This is the minimum you are aiming for. Your book might have twenty chapters and 60,000 words but you need to know before you start whether you have enough information (or can get it by research) to fill the pages of a book.

Planning your Chapters

The best way to know whether your book is worth writing and whether you have the knowledge and information to fill it is to plan the chapters. You might not know exactly what you want in your book or how many chapters it will have, but once you start the planning process you will see if you've got a good idea and whether you are the person to write it.

You can write your chapters out in list form in your notebook or on the computer. If you use the computer, you can move things around and cut and paste chapter information into position. Another trick I use, especially when I am trying to work out the chapter order of a book. is to write each chapter title on a piece of card and jot down its contents. Then I move the cards around (either on the floor or the duvet!) playing with the order to see what should come first, in the middle and last. Once I'm happy with their placing, I number them and head to the computer to write up my chapter list.

Start by working on at least ten chapters. Go through them one by one giving each a title and jotting down what each chapter contains in note-form so for this chapter I wrote something like:

Chapter Fourteen - The Lifestyle Book: finding ideas - enough information - planning chapters - proposals - synopsis - competing books - USPs - audience - biography - sample chapters - sending out a proposal- writing the lifestyle book - promotion - e-books

If you can't fill ten chapters, you won't have enough material for a book but don't despair - your chapter list is a working document until it's sent to a publisher. I go through many permutations before I settle on the final one. New chapters get added in, some chapters get merged and sub-headings get moved about.

Sub-headings are the headings for passages within your book so if you look at my list where it says *planning chapters*, that turned into this section. Each sub-heading will require you to write at least a few sentences on that subject. If you can't manage more than a few lines, it will have to be included under another sub-heading.

Try this Exercise: The Chapter List

Grab a piece of paper and choose a theme - parenting, gardening, computing, interior design, travel or any other lifestyle topic and write this at the top of the page. Come up with a title - don't think about it too much - this is just practice, or use one of these suggestions: *Fashion on a Shoestring, Balcony Gardening, The Holistic Parent, Staying Healthy in your 60s.*

Write the numbers 1 - 10 under your title and now fill in chapter titles that could be included in such a book. How easy is it to come up with chapter titles? Do lots of things spring to mind you could include in such a book? Or does it look a bit on the skinny side?

Every time you come up with an idea, try this exercise - a quick title and suggested chapter headings - to see if you have the makings of a book.

The Proposal

After you have planned out your book, knowing that you will have material for each chapter, you can start thinking about putting together a proposal. Publishers will always ask for a proposal that includes a synopsis, chapter list, information about competing books, your book's unique selling points, your author biography and sample chapters. Publishers differ between how many sample chapters they expect. Some will just look at one, others want at least three.

They may have an electronic proposal system online or you may have to send in your proposal by email. Some publishers have proposal sheets where you fill in the precise information they want and send it back to them by email or hard copy. Use the reference books I mentioned previously to find out which publisher you want to send your proposal to and then look up their website and read their guidelines or details about their submission procedures.

Writing a Synopsis

Your proposal should start with your book title and then be followed by a synopsis of your book. A synopsis is by dictionary definition a brief summary of something. So basically you are summarising what your book is all about in not more than one page of type. Include the overall aim of your book and then refer to the main key points that will appear within your manuscript.

Think of the blurb that you find on the back of a book. Those couple of paragraphs summarise a book's contents and entice the reader to purchase the book or put it down if they're not interested in what it contains. Use your synopsis to entice your publisher and make them want to read more. Give some detail of who this book will appeal to, who you are writing it for and who they could sell it to. Add in details on why this book is unique and what makes it so special readers will want to pick it up. You can also add in the proposed word count and whether illustrations or photographs will be included.

A publisher might also ask you for your strapline. This is basically your synopsis condensed into one sentence. What is your book about? A one-stop guide to roof-top gardening, all you need to know about parenting your teenager or the ultimate guide to travelling in Rome? Try to encapsulate your chosen topic into very few words - not more than ten.

Competing Books

It's very rare that the idea you will come up with has never been written about before. You might have a different slant or a fresh angle but you can bet your lifestyle book will be slotting itself in amongst other books on that subject. In fact, if it doesn't you could have problems. I always thought that if a book had never been published before, it would be snapped up by publishers but it can be just the opposite. If the publisher can't gauge whether readers want your book by the sales of similar titles, they won't take a chance on it.

So you need to look at competing books. Both for your own market research and because the publishers will want to know where your book will sit in relation to similar titles. I use Amazon to see what has been published recently and what the best sellers are. Any information that a publisher may want, like ISBN number, publication date and price, are all available in the book details section on Amazon. And you can see what has been published in a similar vein to your own idea. There's no point in sending a publisher a proposal for a book that is really like one they published last year or using the exact title of another book for your one. This can be a problem in lifestyle books. You want to write about cookery for kids but that's a title that has been used so you'll have to try different permutations and then check to see whether these have been used too. Keep going until you have something unique and original and also check your contents. If your contents is exactly the same as the most recent book on the subject, who is going to want it? Amazon is also good for looking at contents pages so you can see how a subject has been covered and what you can do differently to make your book one that publishers will want to print.

Unique Selling Points

This brings me to unique selling points. What makes your book any different to the millions of other books out there? As I've said, you will be writing in a genre that already exists but your book has got to be unique.

For my book, *The Writer's Internet*, I used the following USPs:

Up-to-date info on how to use the Internet.

A comprehensive guide that covers all aspects of how a writer can use the Internet from finding work to publishing and tutoring.

Written in an easy to read style making it more accessible to non-tech writers.

You don't have to come up with a long list, just two or three points that make your book special. What will make it stand out from the other books that have already been written on the subject? It could be that like my book it makes a subject more accessible to non-experts or beginners. It could contain first-hand experience which is unique to you or it could look at a topic from a new angle containing information that hasn't been covered before. Whatever makes it special, state that in your USPs - publishers want to know they are on to a winner.

Target Audience

You might be asked for information on who your target audience is or who you think will read your book. If you are writing about parenting, that's mums, dads, and grandparents but also educators, teachers, health professionals - think outside of the box as to who else apart from the obvious readership might purchase your book.

If you can find statistics, use them but make sure they are relevant to the country that your publisher prints in. So if you were writing about say, homeschooling, give statistics of the amount of children currently being homeschooled. Or say you are writing about computers; give details of how many homes currently have computers and/or Internet access. Giving a publisher extra information about who your readership is will help them to gauge book sales. And we want plenty of those, don't we?

Author's Biography

You need to tell a publisher all about yourself but in a professional manner. You also need to make your biography relevant to the book proposal that you are sending in. So to begin I start with my general information giving examples of markets I have written for. I include some details on my qualifications and work I am currently undertaking and finish with any previous published books. Depending on what I am using the biography for, I highlight different areas of my work. So for instance, this bio was recently used on a proposal for a book about coaching creative people:

Sarah-Beth Watkins is an experienced freelance writer who has written for various publications over the past 20 years. She has written on a variety of topics including self help, women's development, parenting, health, life coaching topics and NLP. She has also written over 300 articles for the web on a variety of subjects. Her most recent work includes writing articles for Wikio Experts, Overblog, Worldwidehealth.com, New Consciousness Review and for the Wellbeing section of Vista online magazine. Her advice blog can be found at www.sarah-beth.watkins.over-blog.com.

She is a qualified Life Coach and Master NLP Practitioner with certificates in psychology, cognitive behavioural therapy and hypnotherapy. Over the years, she has worked as a mentor and life coach to people from all walks of life.

Sarah-Beth continues to teach creative students in the areas of life writing, article writing and short story writing for The Writer's Academy and creative writing and journalism courses for The Open College.

She is the author of Telling Life's Tales: A Guide to Life Writing for Print and Publication and The Writer's Internet: A Creative Guide to the World Wide Web due out in March 2013 with Compass Books. She is currently completing the manuscript of her third book for Compass, The Lifestyle Writer.

Because this book is about life coaching, I have included information about my life coaching qualifications and the websites that have the most relevant examples of writing on lifestyle coaching subjects.

Whatever topic you are writing about, you need to tailor your biography so that it reflects your expertise and skills in your book's area, making you the best possible person to write your proposed book.

Sample Chapters

As I've mentioned, some publishers want one chapter, others want three. You need to check their guidelines to see how many chapters they expect to be submitted with a proposal. If they want three chapters, they don't have to be in order but I would recommend sending in the first chapter so a publisher can see how you will introduce the book. The other chapters can be whatever you think your best examples are unless the publisher has specifically asked for the first three chapters.

Some writers work on different chapters at different times

working on the most interesting first or the ones they have the most information for. I like to work in a linear fashion because if I left the hardest chapters till last, I'd never get a book finished! But if you feel that your fifth chapter contains the most exciting new information or your eighth chapter reveals something new then work on that one and send it the publishers as part of your proposal package.

Sending out a Proposal

Once you have all the parts of your proposal together in one document and sample chapters to attach, you are ready to send it out to a publisher. You will have done your research by finding out the most appropriate publisher to send it to. Somewhere you need to keep a record so either use a diary, a card file system or a spreadsheet. Keep a note of where and when you sent it and any feedback you receive. Hopefully it will be a book contract but if not, send it out again taking note of any comments that suggest improvement or a different angle. Not all publishers will give you feedback with a rejection but if they do, they could prove useful and might mean you need to do some revising or editing before sending out your proposal again.

Writing the Lifestyle Book

Once you are offered a contract, you are ready to start writing (or if you are writing an e-book, you can just get writing!). Writing a book so often has to fit in with all the other things going on in your life, so you need to plan your writing time or your book's schedule. Your publisher may give you a deadline but if you are asked for an estimation as to when your manuscript will be ready, you need to give them a date that gives you plenty of time.

I manage a chapter a week amongst all the other bits I have to write. Sometimes I'm lucky and get two done, other weeks I'm lucky if I've managed to fit in 1,000 words but a chapter a week will mean that a ten chapter book will be completed in three months, a fifteen chapter book around four months. I always then add on at least a month for editing. And this is only if I know that I have all my research to hand and can begin writing without having to do large amounts of searching for information. If you need to take time to research, you could be looking at a schedule of between six months and a year. It really depends on how much time you can give your book.

Work out your schedule and start writing! You will have some days that are really productive and others that are not so, but if you can work out a rough schedule for your book and stick to it (most of the time) you will have a book together in less than a year.

Doing it Yourself

When your book is written, there is the option of producing it yourself and not using a mainstream publisher. Desk-top publishing is far easier these days and if you only want to produce a few books, then printing them out on your own printer might be an idea. However, if you want to sell your work, you will need an ISBN and if you want a high quality book, you will need to use a professional printer.

There are self-publishing companies you can go to to help produce your book to a high standard but you will have to pay costs. Any way of doing it yourself will involve costs apart from producing your work as an e-book. If you are happy using a computer, can design your own cover and use formatting software then turning your manuscript into an e-book could be the route for you.

E-books

There is an ongoing debate about e-books - some writers love them, some hate them. I wasn't that keen myself until I got a Kindle for Christmas and now I'm hooked. What they do give a writer is the opportunity to produce their own work and have it for sale online. It is a growing market and one writers shouldn't ignore. As I write this, I've just read an article in my Sunday newspaper that said e-book sales outweighed print book sales in the last month. Whatever the statistics say, e-books are here to stay and are becoming increasingly popular.

But why, I hear the dissenters cry! Well, the newer versions of e-book readers have their own backlights so you can read in bed without disturbing your partner. They also have built in wifi so you can download whatever you want to read when you want to read it. Loads of books are available free and you can sample the first few pages of a book before you decide to download it. On the other hand, e-books aren't great to read in the bath, they don't line your walls as well as a bookshelf does and they don't smell nice like the pages of a newly printed book! There are so many pros and cons to e-books that everyone has their own version of whether they are good or bad but they are the future, that's for definite.

E-books can be as simple as a PDF file that you post on a website for people to purchase or download but the more modern e-readers use different file types. Mobicreator is a free software package that can be downloaded from www.mobi pocket.com. It helps with all things to do with formatting and creating your e-book.

One of the easiest ways I have found to create your e-book and have it available to a wide audience is to use Amazon's Kindle Direct Publishing system (www.kdp.amazon.com). It's free to use and to open an Amazon account. They have a free e-book to download *Building Your Book for Kindle* that takes you through the process from formatting your e-book to preparing a cover and entering details about your book. It demystifies the process and makes it easier for writers to have their work available for purchase on the World Wide Web. If you are considering turning your work into an e-book, have a look at this guide. Whether you decide to use Amazon or another e-book website, it will give you lots of valuable information about preparing your manuscript to be read by an e-reader.

Promoting your Work

Whether you produce your own book, turn it into an e-book or send it out to a publisher, you will need to promote it. If you have any contacts in your field of writing, they can be invaluable in promoting your work. Think of people you have worked with, editors you have worked for and contacts you have used to research or interview. Send out any information on your book to them when it is published, including where it can be purchased. Offer review copies to magazines and websites. If you have written for a magazine, tell them too and also suggest that you are available for interview should they want to cover your new title in depth.

Social media is by far the easiest and cheapest way of advertising yourself. Facebook, Twitter and LinkedIn are sites that I use and they are great for sending out messages to your contacts about what you are working on and the details of your book. They are free to use and reach as many friends and contacts as you have but you can also put your account details on the back pages of your book so readers can contact you.

Don't use your personal Facebook page though. I'm sure my readers don't want to see some of the things my friends write about me! You can open a professional page that is attached to your Facebook account. Make sure that your personal page has security settings so that only your friends and family can see your personal information but have your professional page open to the general public. The other great thing about Facebook is that you can sync your Twitter account to it so when you write a post on Facebook, it's also sent out as a tweet. That gets your promotion done twice as fast.

If you have been blogging or writing for a website, ask the web editor if you can run a book promotion online. Of course, if you have your own website or blog then promote away. Create a page that is just about your book and have purchase options available. And talk to people, whether online or in person, the more you spread the word about your book, the more people will be interested in buying your lifestyle book.

Chapter Fifteen

Resources for the Lifestyle Writer

Lifestyle writers can find many resources online from organisations to free reference books and online archives. Have a look at any of the following websites that interest you. You will soon build up your own favourites and find that using the Internet will become a valuable research and information tool.

Organisations and Associations

Below are listed some general writers' websites for organisations and associations that support writers and authors. There are also many organisations that lifestyle writers can join in their specific area of writing but are too numerous to mention here. Whatever your area of writing, browse the Internet for relevant associations to join to keep you up-to-date with the latest trends and developments.

Association of Authors Agents: www.agentassoc.co.uk
Association of Authors and Publishers:
   www.authorsandpublishers.org
Australian Society of Authors: www.asauthors.org
British Guild of Beer Writers: www.beerwriters.co.uk
British Guild of Travel Writers: www.bgtw.org
Circle of Wine Writers: www.winewriters.org
Education Writers Association: www.ewa.org
Garden Writers Association: www.gradenwriters.org
Historical Writers Association: www.thehwa.co.uk
International Women's Writing Guild: www.iwwg.com
Medical Journalists Association: www.mja-uk.org
National Association of Women Writers (USA): www.nasw.org
National Union of Journalists: www.nuj.org.uk

Outdoor Writers Association of America: www.owaa.org

Outdoor Writers and Photographers Guild: www.owpg.org.uk

The Authors Guild (USA): www.authorsguild.org

The Garden Media Guild: www.gardenmediaguild.co.uk

The Guild of Food Writers: www.gfw.co.uk

The Guild of Motoring Writers:
   www.guildofmotoringwriters.co.uk

The Society of American Business Editors and Writers:
   www.sabew.org

The Society of American Travel Writers: www.satw.org

The Society of Authors: www.societyofauthors.org

The Society of Indexers: www.indexers.org.uk

The Society of Medical Writers: www.somw.org

The Writers Guild of America: www.wga.org

The Writers Guild of Canada: www.writersguildofcanada.com

The Writers Guild Of Great Britain: www.writersguild.org.uk

Writers Union of Canada: www.writersunion.ca

Courses for Writers

It never hurts to update your skills or to study in a new area of writing. Here are some course providers that offer a range of courses.

Journalism Classes: www.journalismclasses.com

London School of Journalism: www.lsj.org

National Council for the Training of Journalists, UK:
   www.nctj.com

Open College of the Arts: www.oca-uk.com

The Arvon Foundation: www.arvonfoundation.org

The Publishing Training Centre: www.train4publishing.co.uk

The Travel Writers Classroom: www.travelwritingclass.com

The Writers Academy: www.thewritersacademy.net

The Writers Bureau: www.writersbureau.com

The Writing School:

www.lifestylelearningdirect.com/about_us/writing_school
Writers News Home Study Courses:
www.writers-online.co.uk/home-study

Social Media

If you don't already have social media accounts, it's time to embrace the technological networking world! Check out these websites and start promoting yourself as a writer.

Facebook: www.facebook.com
Twitter: www.twitter.com
LinkedIn: www.linkedin.com
Pinterest: www.pinterest.com

Reference Websites

Whenever you need to fact check, go online and browse these websites. They can help you fill in the blanks and find out background information quickly.

About: www.about.com
All Experts: www.allexperts.com
Answers: www.answers.com
Encyclopedia: www.encyclopedia.com
How Stuff Works: www.howstuffworks.com
Mahalo: www.mahalo.com
Refdesk: www.refdesk.com
Reference: www.reference.com
Wikipedia: www.wikipedia.com

Online Archives

If you need to look for documents and other materials for research, browse some online archives for extra information.

Archive: www.archive.org

Archives Hub: www.archiveshub.ac.uk
Internet Classics Archive: www.classics.mit.edu
The Internet Library of Early Journals: www.bodley.ox.ac.uk
The National Academies Press: www.nap.edu

Free E-books

E-books are great for having reference material to hand on your computer or e-reader. Although you will have to pay for the latest editions or newly published works, there are a lot of websites offering free e-books. Check out:

Amazon: www.amazon.com
Bartleby: www.bartleby.com
Bibliomania: www.bibliomania.com
Book Yards: www.bookyards.com
Free Books: www.freebooks.com
Free E-books: www.free-ebooks.net
Free Book Spot: www.freebookspot.es
Globusz: www.globusz.com
E-book Lobby: www.ebooklobby.com
Online Free E-books: www.onlinefreeebooks.net
Planet E-book: www.planetebook.com
Project Gutenberg: www.gutenberg.org
The E-books Directory: www.e-booksdirectory.com

Happy searching and happy writing!

**COMPASS
BOOKS**

Compass Books focuses on practical and informative 'how-to'
books for writers. Written by experienced authors who also have
extensive experience of tutoring at the most popular creative
writing workshops, the books offer an insight into the more
specialised niches of the publishing game.